100 Questions
(and Answers) About Tests
and Measurement

Q&A SAGE 100 Questions and Answers Series

Neil J. Salkind, Series Editor

1. *100 Questions (and Answers) About Research Methods,* by Neil J. Salkind

2. *100 Questions (and Answers) About Tests and Measurement,* by Bruce B. Frey

3. *100 Questions (and Answers) About Statistics,* by Neil J. Salkind

Visit **sagepub.com/100qa** for a current listing of titles in this series.

100 Questions (and Answers) About Tests and Measurement

Bruce B. Frey
The University of Kansas

Los Angeles | London | New Delhi
Singapore | Washington DC

Los Angeles | London | New Delhi
Singapore | Washington DC

FOR INFORMATION:

SAGE Publications, Inc.

2455 Teller Road

Thousand Oaks, California 91320

E-mail: order@sagepub.com

SAGE Publications Ltd.

1 Oliver's Yard

55 City Road

London EC1Y 1SP

United Kingdom

SAGE Publications India Pvt. Ltd.

B 1/I 1 Mohan Cooperative Industrial Area

Mathura Road, New Delhi 110 044

India

SAGE Publications Asia-Pacific Pte. Ltd.

3 Church Street

#10-04 Samsung Hub

Singapore 049483

Copyright © 2015 by SAGE Publications, Inc.

Printed in the United States of America

ISBN: 978-1-4522-8339-5

Library of Congress Control Number: 2014933224

This book is printed on acid-free paper.

Acquisitions Editor: Vicki Knight

Assistant Editor: Katie Guarino

Editorial Assistant: Yvonne McDuffee

Production Editor: Jane Haenel

Copy Editor: Lana Todorovic-Arndt

Typesetter: C&M Digitals (P) Ltd.

Proofreader: Scott Oney

Indexer: Michael Ferreira

Cover Designer: Candice Harman

Marketing Manager: Nicole Elliott

Certified Chain of Custody
Promoting Sustainable Forestry
www.sfiprogram.org
SFI-01268

SUSTAINABLE FORESTRY INITIATIVE

SFI label applies to text stock

14 15 16 17 18 10 9 8 7 6 5 4 3 2 1

Contents

Preface

We are surrounded by scores. To a large extent in the modern world, we are defined by test performance. For students and teachers, a typical day at school focuses on assessments or preparing for assessment. College students' course work increasingly includes training in measurement, testing, and assessment. Research, especially in the social sciences, depends on valid and reliable measurement to test hypotheses and, as it turns out, to even have a chance at getting statistically significant results.

100 Questions (and Answers) About Tests and Measurement asks (and answers) important questions about the world of social science measurement. It is meant to be an introduction to students new to the concepts, advanced students, and professionals who could use a review of measurement ideas and procedures, and to anyone interested in knowing more about a test they have to take and interpreting the score they will receive.

The questions (and answers) are all numbered and placed in an order that we think makes sense, but you should be able to read any question (and answer) from anywhere in the book and not have to have read anything that came before it. If you are interested in getting more information, though, each answer ends with suggestions for other questions that deal with related topics.

The 100 questions (and answers) are organized into 10 categories so you can find the answer you need quickly and maybe accidentally learn other related stuff while you're at it. The 10 sections are

- The Basics
- Understanding Validity
- Understanding Reliability
- The Statistics of Measurement
- Achievement Tests
- Intelligence Tests
- Personality Tests and Attitude Scales
- Classroom Assessment
- Understanding Test Reports
- Surveys

You'll notice that the book is small and all the questions (and answers) are just a page or two. This is by design so that *100 Questions (and Answers) About Tests and Measurement* can act as a handy, concise reference tool to keep close at hand for whenever measurement problems or concerns rear their thorny heads.

The goal was to provide brief answers that present the most important concepts, procedures, and information. There are likely hundreds more questions that we could have included, but we hope you'll find your most urgent questions asked (and answered) here!

Acknowledgments

Thanks to the editing and production team at SAGE, headed by Vicki Knight, Senior Editor, and Neil Salkind, Series Editor. It has been a pleasant experience thanks to you and your associates. You've all been very nice to me.

Thank you to all of the reviewers for their time and input: Héctor B. Crespo-Bujosa, Carlos Albizu University, San Juan, Puerto Rico; Bruce R. DeForge, University of Maryland Baltimore; Cherisse Y. Flanagan, Abilene Christian University; Jessica C. Hauser, St. Vincent College; Natalie Johnson-Leslie, Arkansas State University; David Oliver Kasdan, Oakland University; William C. Kuba, William Penn University; Karen S. Linstrum, Northwestern Oklahoma State University; Michael J. Ray, The College at Brockport; and Stephanie L. Scifres, Indiana University Purdue University at Columbus.

An additional expression of gratitude goes to members of the production team.

About the Author

Bruce B. Frey, PhD, is an award-winning teacher and scholar at the University of Kansas. His areas of research include classroom assessment and instrument development. Dr. Frey is the author of *Modern Classroom Assessment*, published by SAGE, and *Statistics Hacks*, published by O'Reilly. He also is the coeditor of SAGE's *Encyclopedia of Research Design*. In his spare time, he collects comic books and is especially fond of 1960s DC stories wherein super-pets turn against their superhero masters.

To Mrs. Hank Snow

PART 1

THE BASICS

So, What Is *100 Questions (and Answers) About Tests and Measurement* About?

The world of social science research, statistics, and measurement is complicated. While there are plenty of textbooks, classes to take, online instruction, and learning opportunities available in our modern world, if we are interested in knowing about all that, the material is often aimed just a notch above where we would want it to be. Even "introductory" books or courses may go deeper than many of us need. And in their quest to teach us everything, they often skip over (or, at best, move too quickly through) the basics. This book is designed to answer all of your good questions as you approach a new subject for the first time, or to provide a review of those fundamental concepts, terms, and facts that you were supposed to have mastered way back when. So this book is for the brand-new *and* the not-so-new.

Measurement in the social sciences is a science unto itself. It has its own theories, jargon, strategies, and procedures. The questions and answers chosen for this volume are designed to be understandable. We cover the key stuff you need to know about measurement in ways that assume that you are smart, but didn't happen to have learned any of those things yet.

In the pages ahead, you'll see how *tests* and *measurement* are defined. We aren't talking about how to measure the height of a building or the weight of a diamond. You won't get consumer reviews of the best yardstick to buy. And we aren't talking about how to test your car's ignition system or which pregnancy test is the most accurate. We are talking about the art of quantifying ideas and concepts, ways of producing a number that faithfully reflects whatever nonphysical, abstract, unobservable human trait you want to measure. This book reveals the secrets for making the invisible visible.

More questions? See #2 and #3.

What Exactly Is a Test?

We use the word *test* in many different ways. Waiting for a watched pot to boil might test your patience. Software companies hesitate to release a new product before it has been beta tested. Researchers don't know whether their results are statistically significant until they have conducted a statistical test. We might take a test in school, but sometimes we don't study as hard for it because it isn't a test, it's just a *quiz*. If we examine the use of the word in these different contexts, we can identify some commonalities:

- Tests are made up of procedures.
- Tests produce results that have some meaning.
- Decisions are made based on those results.
- Tests often are big deals for those who are tested because they require some effort, and high-stakes decisions may be made about them.

We will focus on those tests that are administered to people, not products or lab animals, for example. Let's go with this definition:

A test is *an organized set of procedures, questions, or tasks, which produces interpretable quantitative results meant to reflect an individual's level of some characteristic.* (By the way, it turns out there is another scientific definition of a test, which is *the chalky shell of some invertebrates and protozoans.* That is not the definition we will be using in this book.)

In educational and psychological measurement textbooks, tests are often distinguished from assessments. Assessment, we are told, is a process of gathering and analyzing data for the particular purpose of making improvements. Tests are just for the purpose of making a decision. This may be technically correct in a definitional sense, but the reasoning and science underlying all these processes—*testing, assessment,* and (let's throw in) *evaluation*—are the same. And in this book, we won't get hung up on the differences and will tend to use these words interchangeably.

More questions? See #3, #8, and #9.

What Exactly Is Measurement?

*M*easurement is the assignment of numbers to represent quantities, qualities, things, and ideas. In measurement, the assigned number is called a *score,* and its assignment is based on rules. Measurement is a broader term than *test.* A test is a type of measurement, but so is using a sextant to find your way across the ocean. It's fairly easy to measure some quality that is concrete and directly observable like the physical properties of an object, and that type of measurement likely couldn't fill a whole book (e.g., something with a title like *Two Questions and Answers About Weighing Things*). Measuring the abstract and invisible nature of the human mind, concepts like intelligence, knowledge, attitude, and personality, on the other hand, is tougher. This book focuses on the challenge of measuring those abstract human qualities.

It turns out that when assigning a score, that value can carry varying amounts of information. Measurement folks have identified four different types or *levels of measurement,* each providing more information, and allowing more powerful statistical analyses, as one moves "higher":

1. **Nominal.** This word means "in name only," and it refers to the least informative level of measurement where numbers are used only as the names of categories. For example, you might collect data on the hair color of students in a class. While recording that information in a spreadsheet, you might assign a *1* for *blonde,* a *2* for *brown,* a *3* for *red,* and so on. Those scores, though, don't really represent quantities. They are just labels. A score of *3* is not more of anything than a score of *1.*

2. **Ordinal.** At this level, the scores indicate some order in terms of "how much" there is of something. In a footrace, the fastest runner might receive a *1* for first place, the next fastest gets a *2,* and so on. There is more information than at the nominal level, but the distance between scores in terms of whatever is being measured (speed in this case) is unknown. It doesn't make any sense to average these numbers, for example.

3. **Interval.** Here the numbers have real quantitative meaning. They reflect an exact amount of something. "Interval" refers to the fact that there are equal amounts of difference in quantity between any two adjacent scores. The scales used for temperature, Celsius or Fahrenheit thermometers, for example, are at the interval level. Most statistical analyses, like averaging and calculating variability, are allowed at this level of measurement.

4. **Ratio.** This level of measurement is interval scaling without any negative numbers allowed. With a thermometer, which is at the interval level, scores below 0 are allowed. The 0 is arbitrary, though, and does not represent the complete absence of something. At the ratio level, though, there is a true 0. Nothing is below it. The simple counting of objects is measurement at the ratio level. Your aunt might have zero cats, but she cannot have less than zero cats. It is named "ratio" level, by the way, because the use of ratios and proportions now makes sense. Your aunt can have twice as many cats as her neighbor, but we don't often talk about it being half as cold today as yesterday.

More questions? See #2 and #62.

Most of the Ways I Can Think of to Measure Something Seem Pretty Straightforward. What Are the Important Differences Between Measuring Something Like Weight and Something More Abstract Like Knowledge?

Measurement in education and psychology differs from measurement in the physical sciences like physics and engineering in one important way. The object of measurement, the thing for which you wish to assign a score representing quantity, is abstract and can't be seen. It might not even exist! These invisible traits and human characteristics that we social scientists wish to measure are called **constructs**.

A construct (pronounced CON-struct) is not directly observable. It is a conceptual, intangible variable that a test maker has built and defined (thus, the term *construct*) intellectually through the application of theory and research. The job of the test developer is to find ways to make these unseen constructs observable. Typical strategies for assessing constructs are

- **Asking questions**

  This is the most traditional way of finding out what's going on inside our heads.

- **Observing behaviors**

  We can't see thoughts, but we can see behavior.

- **Assigning performance tasks**

  Evaluators from classroom teachers to work supervisors make judgments about our skills, abilities, and personality traits by looking at the work we produce.

Because we cannot see constructs, the quality of social science measurement depends to a large extent on how well the scores on a test really reflect the construct of interest. These issues of validity are discussed in Questions #7 and #8.

Some of the constructs that are common measurement goals and are discussed in this book include knowledge, ability, skill, intelligence, potential college success, personality, attitude, depression, and alcoholism. See how these are different variables, in terms of measurement, than height, weight, speed, or thickness? The art of measurement in the social sciences is the opposite of the stage magician's art. Instead of making things disappear, test makers make things appear.

More questions? See #8 and #17.

What Are Some of the Different Types of Tests, and How Are They Used?

The tests covered in this book are all designed to assign a score to humans. The scores are meant to quantify levels of invisible traits called *constructs*. All the constructs associated with the tests we are interested in are within the minds of people and can't be seen directly. They are reflections of how we feel, what we can do, and what we know. These are the tests of education and psychology. There are three major types of educational and psychological measures. They differ in their intended purposes, why we use them, and the nature of the constructs they measure.

Most tests in the world of education can be classified as **achievement tests**. These are the tests that measure knowledge and understanding of the information and skills we learn in school. The format of achievement tests varies from the short and informal, like when a teacher calls on a student to answer a question, to the somewhat important, such as that big midterm chemistry exam, to the high-stakes intensity of a 3-hour, standardized college admissions test. Major achievement tests include the *SAT*, the *ACT*, and the *Graduate Record Exam* (GRE).

Another use of testing is to measure ability in order to predict or estimate how well one will perform in school or on the job. The general category name for tests that predict the future is **aptitude tests**. By far the most common type of aptitude test in both education and psychology is the **intelligence test**. Intelligence tests are meant to assess those abilities that correlate with success in school, on the job, and while living independently in the world. Major intelligence tests include the *Wechsler Intelligence Scale for Children* (WISC), the *Woodcock-Johnson Tests of Cognitive Abilities*, the *Kaufman Assessment Battery for Children* (K-ABC), and the *Stanford-Binet Intelligence Scale*.

A third type of test in the world of psychology and, sometimes, in education, is broadly labeled as a **personality test**. These measures are designed to score our feelings, our attitudes, and how our minds work. Sometimes the constructs are well-defined complex mental illnesses. Other times, personality tests have less complicated lower-stakes goals, such as measuring how you feel about a company's new line of baked beans. Major tests in this category, such as the *Minnesota Multiphasic Personality Inventory* (MMPI), assess personality types and disorders or are used to diagnose problems, like depression or addiction to alcohol and other drugs.

Other questions and answers in this book explore the characteristics of these tests that are necessary for them to be useful and examine how the scores from these measures are used and interpreted. These methods of test development and application are essentially the same for all educational and psychological tests, whether they are meant to measure achievement, assess intelligence and aptitude, or identify personality and attitude.

More questions? See #4 and #7.

What Are the Different Ways to Interpret a Test Score?

There are really only two ways that a score on a test can mean anything:

1. The score can be interpreted by comparing it to the scores of others. Is it higher, lower, or about average compared with other folks who took the same test? And how much higher or lower compared with others is it? This approach, which gives meaning to a score by understanding what sort of scores normal people (if you'll excuse the expression) get, is called *norm-referenced*. What is important in this approach is whether a score is above or below average.

2. The score can be interpreted by understanding what the score directly represents in terms of the level of some trait, which chunk of knowledge has been learned, how well a skill has been mastered, the presence or absence of some condition, and so on. This approach doesn't care how one's performance compares with other people, but instead interprets a score against some external criteria or standards. Under this *criterion-referenced* approach, everyone who is measured might get the exact same score or be in the same category of performance. It is not important whether a score is above or below average.

As an example, pretend you just ran a mile-long race against six other people. You finished the mile in 4 minutes and 36 seconds. (I said we were pretending.) This score of 276 seconds ($(4 \times 60) + 36$) can be interpreted in two different ways.

If you interpreted your performance in a norm-referenced way, you'd be interested in whether you were first or last, whether you won the race, and who you'd beat. (Notice how even calling the mile run a "race" is consistent with a norm-referenced philosophy.)

If you interpreted your running time in a criterion-referenced way, you would be more interested in what a score of 276 seconds says about you and your abilities. For instance, a speed that fast likely indicates that you are very healthy. It also probably means that you have mastered the ability to run. The score itself has meaning without knowing how others scored.

College admissions tests such as the ACT, SAT, MCAT, and GRE, and sometimes the grades one gets in school, are assigned and interpreted in a norm-referenced way.

"State tests" like those required in U.S. schools by No Child Left Behind legislation are usually criterion-referenced. They are designed to categorize students based on their levels of achievement.

A few simple questions will tell you whether scores are norm-referenced or criterion-referenced. Might everyone get the same score? If so, it is criterion-referenced. To understand the score, do you have to know how other people scored? If so, it is norm-referenced.

More questions? See #8, #17, and #86.

What Are the Different Ways to Judge Whether a Test Is Any Good?

The quality of a test is really a matter of the value of the scores that are produced by that test. There are two essential characteristics of scores that make them useful:

- The scores reflect the construct of interest. The *construct* is the invisible trait that one wishes to measure, such as knowledge, depression, or intelligence. A test is only "good" if it produces scores that are directly related to the actual level or *amount* of the construct. **Validity** is the characteristic of test scores that measure what they are supposed to measure.

- The scores are consistent for an individual. The scores produced by a test are almost always used to make decisions or judgments about individuals, so they need to represent the typical score each individual would get. This means that there should be very little randomness in people's responses to test items and questions. If a student misses a question that she would normally get correct just because a noisy truck rolled by or because she happened to skip breakfast that day, that affects the consistency of her score. It is a slightly different score than it should be and is, therefore, less *precise*. **Reliability** is the characteristic of test scores that are consistent and precise.

There are two different ways, then, to judge whether a test is any good or not. Is it valid? Is it reliable?

Measurement folks would want me to be clear that it is the test scores that are valid or reliable, not the test itself. This makes sense because a single test can be used for different purposes with different people in different environments and could demonstrate different levels of validity and reliability across those different contexts.

The validity of a test is generally considered *the* most important quality in judging its value. So much meaning is assigned to the numbers produced by tests and so much faith is placed in those scores that it is a serious problem if they do not mean what they are assumed to mean. Imagine a test for depression that actually measures whether a person is getting enough sleep or a measure of intelligence that doesn't work well for those whose first language is not English. Treatment strategies, placements in educational programs, college admissions, research findings, job hires—all depend on the assumption that tests measure what they are supposed to measure.

Reliability is also important in judging the quality of a test. Notice, though, that a test can be reliable without being valid. Reliability is ensured as long as people get the typical score that they would get on the instrument, regardless of whether that instrument measures what it is supposed to. A "math" test that actually requires high-level reading skills in order to do well might be very reliable, but it probably doesn't work well when used to measure math ability.

More questions? See #8 and #17.

PART 2

UNDERSTANDING VALIDITY

What Does It Mean to Say That a Test Is Valid?

Question #7 introduced and described the concept of validity. It is the quality of a test that measures what it is supposed to. There are many ways, though, that one could argue that the scores from a particular test do indeed represent the "thing" that they are supposed to.

Generally speaking, there are four types of arguments, four categories of evidence that can support a claim of validity. You can think of these categories as four types of validity, if you'd like, though hardcore measurement experts believe that validity is validity, and while one can use a variety of strategies to develop different lines of reasoning for a conclusion of validity, there really aren't different "types." A test is either useful for its intended purpose or it is not. For those, however, who like to categorize, the four common types of validity evidence are

- **Content Validity Evidence**

  Arguments that present a listing or table of a well-defined domain or category and examine whether the actual questions, items, or tasks on a test fairly represent those areas are content validity arguments. If the test "covers what it is supposed to," then it has content validity.

- **Criterion Validity Evidence**

  Some tests are designed for the specific purpose of predicting or estimating performance on some other test or criterion. Criterion validity for these sorts of tests can be demonstrated by presenting evidence, usually statistical evidence, that scores from the test do correlate with scores on the other measure.

- **Construct Validity Evidence**

  A *construct* is the measurement term for that invisible abstract quality or trait that a test is designed to measure. It is what the score is supposed to represent. So, any argument that refers to that trait and uses theory or data or statistical analyses to demonstrate that there is a connection between score and construct can be thought of as construct validity evidence. If that definition sounds a lot like our general definition of validity, you are right. That's why many measurement theorists believe that all validity evidence is construct validity evidence, and there are not different types of validity.

- **Consequential Validity Evidence**

  This is the most modern of the traditional strategies for demonstrating test validity. Consequential validity arguments go beyond simply arguing that the scores on a test do represent the construct of interest. They point out that a test is designed for a specific purpose, and if the overall intended purpose of the test is not being fulfilled, then the test is not valid. Sometimes this is called *social consequences validity.* For example, a claim that the use over the years of a particular classroom behavior test has resulted in a disproportionate number of boys being identified as having attention deficit/hyperactivity disorder (ADHD) would be a consequential validity issue.

  More questions? See #17, #28, and #40.

What Is Content Validity, Why Is It Important, and How Is It Established?

*C*ontent *validity* is the characteristic of a test that is made up of items that fairly represent all the items that could be on the test. For a standardized achievement test, do the questions represent all the traditional academic areas that are considered important, such as reading, writing, and mathematics? For a teacher-made classroom assessment, does each task relate to an important instructional objective? Does the test "cover what was taught"? For a psychological or personality test, are all the key distinguishing characteristics of a particular disorder or trait accounted for in the questions asked?

Content validity is important because it demonstrates that the abstract construct, that invisible trait or variable one wishes to measure (see Question #3), has been operationalized in a reasonable way. In order to make an invisible trait observable, concrete questions must be answered or specific tasks must be performed. (Educational and psychological measurement is, after all, a *behavioral* science.) Those questions or tasks must reflect a proper breakdown or organizational scheme that has defined the construct by domains, or subdomains, or groups of behaviors. We must have a tangible definition of what the trait looks like when we see it. A test with good content validity produces scores that allow us to "see" the construct.

Tests with well-established content validity usually begin with an actual list or table that has detailed the material elements of a construct. This list might come from a professional organization that has established knowledge standards or skill competencies for practicing members of their profession. It might come from an accepted theory or research study that has identified components of a personality trait or illness that should be included on any valid assessment. It might come from a classroom teacher who has designed a *table of specifications* for what the final should cover and how much weight should be given to each topic.

Most arguments about validity focus on the test score itself. Content validity arguments, though, focus on the content of the test, the items and questions themselves. Are the questions a fair representation of the questions that should be on the test?

More questions? See #40 and #71.

What Is Criterion Validity, Why Is It Important, and How Is It Established?

*C*riterion validity* is the characteristic of a test that produces scores correlated with some other measure. Usually, an actual correlation coefficient, a statistic that quantifies the size and nature of relationships between variables (see Question #28), is produced as the evidence of the strength of relationship between the two sets of scores, though other research findings can be used to establish a relationship. For example, the makers of a college admissions test would want to show that scores on their measure correlate with performance in college, perhaps the grade point average after freshman year. Developers of a schoolwide test given at the start of the year meant to predict performance on statewide math tests that will be taken at the end of the year would be expected to demonstrate a strong relationship between their scores and the eventual state test scores. New versions of accepted tests, such as personality tests or intelligence tests, which want to offer their assessments as valid substitutes, argue that scores from their tests correlate well with the "gold standard" instruments they wish to replace.

Criterion validity is important to establish for tests that predict the future or estimate concurrent performance on some other test. These two aspects of criterion validity are treated as two separate validity arguments, **predictive criterion validity** and **concurrent criterion validity**.

Research studies are usually required to establish criterion validity. Test developers or those who are studying the validity of a test form a sample of test takers, and they have them take both measures or collect the data for the two measures in some way. Then, a correlation coefficient is calculated between the two sets of scores. Usually, a high correlation is hoped for to support criterion validity claims. Depending on the actual claims about the construct being measured, however, one might hope for a moderate correlation, a low correlation, or even no relationship at all. For example, if I have a new, hip way to define and assess intelligence, I'd want to demonstrate that my measure correlates somewhat with other intelligence tests, not so high that it suggests I'm not doing anything new, but not so low that it suggests I'm not measuring intelligence at all.

Criterion validity focuses on the test score itself. Does it really reflect the intended construct? If so, it should correlate with other tests that supposedly measure the same construct.

More questions? See #40 and #51.

What Is Construct Validity, Why Is It Important, and How Is It Established?

*C*onstruct validity can be defined in two ways, depending on whether one is in a broad, philosophical mood or one wants a more concrete, applied definition. Broadly speaking, and consistent with the thinking of measurement experts and modern textbooks, all validity is construct validity. That is, construct validity is usually defined as the characteristic of a test with scores that reflect the construct (invisible trait) a test is intended to measure. But that's really the same definition we use for *validity* in general. So, a way of thinking called the *unitary view of validity* treats all validity arguments as construct validity arguments and argues that it is not useful, or worse, misleading, to talk about different types of validity. The other approach to defining construct validity is just fine with categorizing validity arguments into "types," such as *content validity* and *criterion validity*. This book is comfortable with talking about types of validity and treats those validity arguments that refer to theory about the nature of a construct or the conceptual definition of a construct as *construct validity* arguments.

Construct validity is important for all types of tests (as it is the central requirement of all tests), but it is particularly emphasized for those tests designed to measure very abstract or complex variables. It is also particularly important for tests that measure controversial constructs. For example, traits such as intelligence, depression, addiction, autism, attention deficit disorder, and cognitive disabilities can be defined in different ways, and they all have political and socially sensitive histories and culturally distinct definitions. Any test that purports to measure one of these sorts of constructs needs to provide a very strong and comprehensive body of construct validity evidence.

Construct validity arguments usually are built from a mix of types of evidence. Theory typically provides the framework and backbone for construct validity arguments. Research findings showing that scores "behave" the way they are supposed to can be used to support construct validity claims. And, because construct validity is the broad umbrella concept for all of validity, evidence of criterion validity and content validity is often used to make construct validity arguments.

How do you know that the score from a test actually reflects what it is supposed to? Answer that question, and you have established construct validity.

More questions? See #50 and #60.

What Is Consequential Validity, Why Is It Important, and How Is It Established?

*C*onsequential validity, or social consequences validity, is concerned with the unintended social consequences from the use of a test. It fits with a broader definition of validity than the one that has been traditionally applied.

You'll recall that validity, as usually defined, is something along the lines of "whether a test measures what it is supposed to." More precisely, validity is the extent to which the *scores* from a test reflect the intended construct. Under that widely accepted understanding of the term, the unintended social consequences of test use, while important to consider, do not affect the validity of a test. A couple of decades back, however, the official standards for measurement supported by the various interested professional organizations, such as the *American Educational Research Association* and the *American Psychological Association*, provided an expanded view of validity as referring to the extent to which a test is useful for its *intended purpose*. And if a test is intended to help society and help the people who are being tested, then consequential validity should be a concern.

To explore whether a test has established consequential validity, one must consider several different social implications of test use:

- What actions are triggered after a score is obtained for an individual? What happens above or below certain high or low "cut scores"?
- What are the intrinsic social values implicit (or explicit) in the use of the test? How does society view high or low IQ scores or performance on the SAT, for example?
- Are students "labeled" for many years (and, maybe, for life) and placed in categories or tracks from which there is no escape, even if one would no longer correctly belong in the category if he or she was tested again?
- Are the technical qualities of the test (in terms of reliability and traditional validity standards) high enough that use of the test is ethical?
- Is there evidence of bias toward identifiable groups in the use of the test?
- What are the legal consequences of identification or placement resulting from the test's use?

More questions? See #13 and #14.

What Does It Mean to Say a Test Is Biased?

Parents, students, teachers, doctors, patients, employers, job applicants, test makers, researchers—all types of stakeholders in the world of test and measurement—pretty much mean the same thing when they worry that a test might be *biased*. They mean that the test is unfair toward a particular group.

If the test is supposed to measure a "good" thing, like intelligence or achievement, a biased test produces lower scores for members of the group. If the test is supposed to measure a "bad" thing, like aggression or attention deficit disorder, a biased test produces higher scores for that group. (Bias can also occur in directions that actually improve performance for the affected group, but test takers aren't usually concerned about that sort of bias.)

The bias comes in the systematic nature of the errors that a test makes when producing scores for test takers with some demographic characteristic of interest. Tests that make random errors, as opposed to consistent, systematic errors, are not considered biased. (Those tests suffer from low reliability, but aren't, by definition, *biased*.)

Frequently, there is an important difference between those who take tests and those who make tests in terms of what evidence is necessary to conclude that a test is biased. Consider, for example, a high school achievement test that measures mathematical ability. There is sometimes found to be a gap in performance between males and females, with males scoring a little bit higher on standardized math tests than females. Some would take this disparity in performance on these tests as evidence that the test is biased. Test developers, however, don't usually treat the mere existence of group differences as evidence of test bias. Instead, they have a somewhat more complex, but fairly clever, requirement. Get two large groups of males and females and have them all take the test. Within those large groups, choose a bunch of males and a bunch of females who scored about the same on the total test. Then, look at each question on the test and see how well it predicts performance overall (which is assumed to be the best estimate of ability). Look at this relationship for males and then for females. If the relationship between the item and the total score is different (in strength) for one group compared with the other, then one can conclude that that *question* might be biased. Individual items are often identified as potentially biased in this way and removed from tests to ensure that the test as a whole is not biased.

More questions? See #14, #19, and #20.

What Does Evidence of Test Bias Look Like?

To measurement scientists, *bias* means that a test systematically assigns the wrong scores to individuals who are members of an identifiable demographic group, such as race, ethnicity, or gender. Bias is particularly harmful when members of a group receive lower scores than they should on high-stakes assessments such as college admissions tests, intelligence tests, and job aptitude tests. To use the technical language of the field, a test is biased when it displays *differential validity*. It is accurate and fair for some groups, but not for others. There are several types of evidence or arguments that can demonstrate test bias.

Evidence can focus on the items or questions on a test. If two different groups who otherwise have the same ability or knowledge differ in whether they get a particular item correct, that can be evidence of bias for that item. Sometimes the content of the questions can reflect stereotyping or cultural bias, which might disadvantage some group. For example, math questions that refer to investments in mutual funds might only make sense to those whose family income is such that they talk about retirement strategies around the dinner table. The idea is that this question might be valid for measuring mathematics ability for some, but not for others. That's differential validity.

Another argument for the presence of test bias centers on the underlying *construct* (such as ability, intelligence, skill, personality trait) that a test is designed to measure. Is the construct the same for different groups? The evidence for these arguments is usually correlational. Do scores on this test correlate with scores on other similar measures in the same way? For example, if scores on a college admissions test (e.g., SAT or ACT) correlate with grades in the first year of college pretty well for white students, but not so well for Native American students, then that test is demonstrating differential validity. Sometimes a construct-based argument is made by looking at the correlations among the parts within a test. Imagine an intelligence test that is meant to measure two different constructs, for example, such as verbal ability and problem-solving skills. The items on the verbal ability subtest should correlate well with each other and not so well with items on the problem-solving skills subtest. This would likely be a basic overall validity requirement. What if, though, there is a nice pattern of these expected correlations for girls, but not for boys? That suggests that the test measures somewhat different constructs for different genders. That's differential validity. And that's evidence of test bias.

More questions? See #19 and #20.

Some Types of Validity Evidence Must Be More Important for Some Types of Tests, but Not Important for Other Types of Tests. What's the General Strategy for Making an Argument for the Validity of a Test?

There are four aspects of validity discussed in this book (see Questions #9, #10, #11, and #12). *Content validity* is the extent to which a test includes items that are a fair representation of all the items that could be on the test. *Criterion validity* focuses on how well scores on a test correlate with scores on another test that is supposed to measure the same thing. *Construct validity* is the broad requirement that scores should reflect a particular construct. *Consequential validity* is concerned with whether the consequences for those who take a test, regardless of their score, is as intended.

While all types of validity are important for all social science measurement, and some measurement folks treat validity as a unitary concept that doesn't have different "types" (see Question #11), different categories of tests would be expected to emphasize different aspects of validity. Different validity types are reasonably perceived as more important, depending on the purpose of the test.

Tests that are meant to measure knowledge of a well-established and organized knowledge base, such as classroom exams and statewide school tests, need to establish that their items represent that knowledge base well, so content validity is important. College admissions tests and other measures that claim to predict or estimate performance in some other domain are expected to provide, at a minimum, evidence of criterion validity. Intelligence tests and other psychological tests that measure subjective and, perhaps, controversially defined traits that derive from comprehensive theories of human behavior go to great lengths to justify the definitions of their measurement targets. These tests go to great lengths to construct validity evidence. The fourth type of validity argument, consequential validity, is particularly important for placement tests. The scores from placement tests are used to assign test takers to particular "tracks" or programs. For instance, placement tests are used on the job, as people enter college, and in special education. The consequences concern relates to whether people benefit from that placement. Consequential validity also becomes an issue when tests are evaluated for bias. If members of different races, ethnicities, or genders are more or less likely to receive different placements, over time does that have a positive or negative effect on society?

This table shows different types of tests and the aspect of validity that might be considered most crucial to establish:

	Content	Criterion	Construct	Consequential
Achievement Tests	X			
College Admissions Tests		X		
Intelligence and Personality Tests			X	
Placement Tests				X

More questions? See #7, #8, and #26.

I Need to Build a Test. How Can I Make Sure It Is Valid?

There is a series of steps that we can follow if our goal is to build a test and have faith in its validity when all is said and done. The process begins with construct definition and ends with a final instrument that can be revised and improved over time. Here are the procedures for valid test development:

1. **Identify a construct or constructs.**

   Decide what you want to measure. Are you hoping to measure attitude for a research study? Are you a classroom teacher who needs to assess whether instructional objectives are being met? Do you need to predict success in your community college?

2. **Define your construct(s).**

   There are two ways you need to define whatever it is you wish to measure:

   a. Put words around the abstract concept you wish to measure until you have created a dictionary-type definition. *What is the nature of intelligence? What level of understanding do you wish for your students? Is depression the same thing as anger?*

   b. Create a test blueprint. By producing a table of specifications that identifies the domains, subdomains, or areas and categories, and the relative weight in terms of number of items for each, you will know the pieces that will make up your test.

3. **Design questions, items, or tasks that make your construct visible.**

   What behaviors or type of responses will indicate presence of the abstract characteristic you wish to measure? How can you make the construct observable?

4. **Write a large number of items or tasks.**

   Create a larger pool than you think you will need, so later you can pick the most valid items for your final draft.

5. **Design a scoring system.**

   Is your test made up of right or wrong questions that can be scored with 1's and 0's for each item? Is performance more subjective and a scoring rubric, which allows for a range of scores based on the nature of responses, would be most valid?

6. **Test the test.**

   Give your items to a large group of people who represent the intended population for your test and study the results.

7. **Choose those items that increase validity.**

   Which items, statistically, seem to do the best job of measuring your construct? Does the wording and format of each item work well for your study sample?

8. **Build a final test with the best items.**

9. **Continue to collect data on how your test performs.**

   Even after you have finished the "final" version of your test, you may wish to improve and revise it over time.

More questions? See #8, #17, #60, and #71.

PART 3

UNDERSTANDING RELIABILITY

What Is Reliability, and How Is It Different From Validity?

*R*eliability is the characteristic of a test that produces consistent scores. Scores are reliable if each individual who takes the test receives a score that represents typical performance for that individual. This differs from validity because reliability only refers to whether the score is the average score that person should receive on the test. Reliability tells us nothing about what construct that score represents; that's the purview of validity.

The classic definition of reliability, as defined as part of the 100-year-old measurement theory known as *classical test theory*, is that it is the proportion of variability in a set of scores that is not random. Reliability is often expressed with a number that is an estimate of that proportion. Imagine that you could give a test to an individual an infinite number of times. Scores for that person would vary a bit around some true mean level of performance. Sometimes the scores would be a bit higher than that individual's average or typical score, and sometimes they would be a bit lower. That theoretical average score is called the *true score* in classical test theory. The extent to which actual obtained scores vary around each person's true score is reliability. A reliable test produces a group of actual scores that are very close to that group's true scores.

Test scores are almost always wrong to some extent. Sometimes the error in a test score is systematic. That is, it misses the mark to some degree for everyone who takes the test in any situation. Systematic error is a validity concern. A test might be so poorly designed that the scores do not represent the construct of interest.

Notice that such a test might still be reliable. A test taker might get the exact same score every time he or she takes the test because it has perfect reliability, but the test never measures the right thing. That would be a serious validity problem.

Sometimes the error in a test score is random and unsystematic. It occurs by chance. You might respond to questions on an attitude survey without paying much attention and accidentally circle "strongly agree" instead of "strongly disagree." The next day you might have been more careful. You might guess the answer to a multiple-choice question and get lucky. On another occasion, you might have been less fortunate and guessed wrong. These sorts of random events affect the scores people get on tests. Reliable tests are designed to decrease the amount and magnitude of these random errors.

When we read about the quality of tests or ask questions about whether they are any good or not, we often use the phrase "valid and reliable" all together as if the two terms mean the same thing. You can see how they are two different, but equally important, criteria for useful measurement.

More questions? See #8 and #18.

What Are the Different Types of Reliability?

The reliability of test scores refers to the consistency of those scores. Consequently, different ways of estimating reliability represent different ways of defining and calculating "consistency." One can think of consistency between administrations, consistency in performance across items within the test, consistency between two different scorers, and consistency between two different forms of the same test.

Consistency between administrations is called *test-retest reliability*. The idea is that if the scores from a test aren't random, but actually represent something, giving the test twice without much time in between should produce roughly the same scores. This is a practical way of trying to demonstrate that an individual's score represents the typical score he or she would get on a measure. We can't give the test an infinite number of times and average them, of course, to really know what a typical score would be, but we could give it twice and correlate those scores to estimate reliability.

If you are interested in *internal reliability*, whether responses to some of the items are consistent with responses to the other items, then you can compute a number that represents the correlation of all the items with each other. If a bunch of items are combined to form a total single score, then one would hope that all the items measure something similar. Internal reliability is the most commonly reported estimate of consistency because a test developer can use data from a single test administration.

If the scoring on a test is subjective, then it requires some human judgment, and those judgments can be inconsistent between judges. The type of reliability that is interested in the subjectivity of the scoring of a test is *inter-rater reliability*. If the scoring comes from observation, this type of reliability is sometimes called *inter-observer reliability*. Evidence of inter-rater reliability is sometimes in the form of a percentage of agreement between two raters on what the score should be. Sometimes it is reported as a correlation between the scores of two different raters.

The fourth type of reliability is unique to the concerns of large-scale test developers. They often conceive of their "test" as a large pool of items that have been developed and validated. They can choose items from this pool to produce different forms of the same test. This way, if you retake the ACT because you didn't like your score the first time, you won't see the same questions you saw before. Test developers use *parallel forms reliability* to demonstrate that there is consistency across forms. Among some other criteria, parallel forms reliability requires that all forms are equal in difficulty.

As with validity, which type of reliability evidence is relevant depends on the purpose of the test and the nature of the scoring. Computer scored tests, for example, will have (nearly) perfect inter-rater reliability, so there is no need to calculate it. And tests that don't have more than one version cannot demonstrate parallel forms reliability.

More questions? See #7, #17, and #24.

If the Traditional Way of Thinking About Reliability Is Called the Classical Theory, That Suggests There Is a More Contemporary Way of Thinking About Things. What Has Come Since?

Classical test theory or *true score theory* is interested in examining the reliability of a group of items that have been combined to form a single scale and are meant to be summed in some way to create a single total score. It assumes that the reliability of a test's scores and the associated average amount of random error in those scores is constant and the same for all individuals regardless of their ability. While the basic definition of reliability as "the proportion of observed score variance that is not random" has not changed in the 100 years or so since classical test theory has been with us, a more comprehensive analysis of reliability has developed starting in the late 1960s, which takes into account a greater amount of information about a testing situation, especially information about the person taking the test. This new theory is called modern test theory or **item response theory**.

Item response theory is most commonly used with achievement tests (with their 0 for *wrong* and 1 for *right* scoring systems) but can be used for any sort of educational or psychological testing. Using the procedures derived from the theory, one looks at each item score (the response to an item) in relationship to the ability level of the individual answering the item and estimates the probability that someone with a given level of ability would get a question correct. For a given individual, the most reliable item, statistically speaking, is one that matches his or her level of ability perfectly. A good match, if one wants to learn about someone's ability, is an item where we aren't sure whether they will get it correct or not. So, items an individual has a 50% chance of getting correct based on our ability estimates are informative items for that individual.

This may sound pretty complex and maybe even a bit irrational. After all, if we know someone's ability level, we don't need to test her. But a good test developed under item response theory is full of items that are informative across a range of abilities and perform especially well for the average ability level in the intended testing population. Data is collected during test development so that item responses across a range of abilities are known for each question. For each item, a curve can be graphed, which shows the probability of getting an item correct across the whole range of ability levels. For a good item, its *item characteristic curve* shows that those with high ability (as estimated, usually, by total test score) are very likely to get the question correct, those with low ability are very unlikely to get the question right, and those with average ability are 50% likely to get the question correct.

Under item response theory, each item has a certain amount of reliability as shown on these item characteristic curves. Tests made up of many items with high reliability produce total scores that are highly reliable.

In the digital age, many tests are now taken on computers. By applying item response theory, and relying on a large database of items to choose from, *computer adaptive tests* are possible. These allow for customized tests to be built on the fly for test takers. Computer adaptive testing systems estimate ability based on performance on the first few items on the test and then choose items that are as reliable as possible for each person individually.

More questions? See #14 and #20.

What Are the Important Differences Between Classical and Item Response Theory?

Item response theory differs from classical test theory in several important ways. The differences are based on the assumptions about reliability itself and the way information is generated to analyze items.

Some of the key differences between classical test theory and item response theory are summarized in this table:

Classical Test Theory	Item Response Theory
Estimating reliability requires a study with a small number of people (about 30) whose individual characteristics don't matter.	Estimating reliability requires a study with a large number of people (many hundreds) with a wide variety of abilities.
Reliability estimates focus on the total score of a test.	Reliability estimates focus on the amount of "information" in each individual item on the test.
There is a single reliability estimate that is applied to everyone who takes the test.	Tests have different "reliabilities" for different people.
The standard error of measurement is the same for each observed score. (See Question #92.)	The standard error of measurement is different for each observed score.
The best strategy for producing a reliable test is to use many items. Reliable tests tend to be very long.	The best strategy for producing a reliable test is to choose items reliable for each test taker. Reliable tests can be very short.
Item difficulty and discrimination are represented by single numbers, which are averages across the test-taking population. (See Questions #36 and #37.)	Item difficulty and discrimination are represented by functions or curves, which differ based on the ability level of each test taker.
Everyone takes the same test.	With computer adaptive tests, everyone takes a test with a set of items customized just for them. (See Question #19.)

More questions? See #19 and #33.

What Does Internal
Reliability Look Like?

Reliability is defined as the proportion of variance in scores that is *true score* variance. True score is the average score you would get on a test if you took it an infinite number of times. The need for a concept like true score arises because of the realization that each time a person is asked a question, there will be some inconsistency in how he or she responds. This is true for attitude items and personality assessment, where how you feel in the morning might be slightly different than how you feel in the afternoon, and this is true for achievement tests where whether you "know" an answer, or can't remember it just now, or make a lucky guess, will all depend on, to some degree, how lucky you are in the moment. To deal with this expected random "error," good tests are made up of many items, not just one or two. The thinking is that while there may be a little unpredictable imprecision for any given item's response in one direction or the other, across a bunch of items, those errors will cancel themselves out, and the total score will be reliable. This requires that all the questions that are on a single scale (a group of items meant to measure the same thing) do correlate well with each other. It is important that items summed together to produce one score measure the same construct. The degree to which all the items on a single scale are related to each other is *internal reliability*.

Question #30 presents these responses to items on an attitude scale for three different people:

Respondent	Item 1	Item 2	Item 3	Item 4	Total Score
Washington	4	4	5	2	15
Adams	1	3	1	1	6
Jefferson	3	2	4	2	11

Let's examine the internal consistency of these four items. There are statistical ways to estimate internal reliability (e.g., Questions #30, #31, and #32), but let's just eyeball it for now. Assume that these attitude items had answer options ranging from *1, Strongly Disagree*, to *5, Strongly Agree*. We want to know if people respond consistently across items. In other words, for each individual, does the answer for Item 1 predict the answer on Item 2 and other items? Does each person tend to answer around a 4, for instance, for every item or a 3 for every item?

What we don't care about is the total scores and whether they vary (which they do; they range from 6 to 15). We also can't look at the "internal consistency" of any single item. Internal reliability only applies to consistency in responses within a group of items. So, in our data, did Washington tend to answer about the same across items? Was Adams consistent? What about Jefferson? While the three certainly varied from each other, they were pretty consistent within themselves. Even though scores vary within each column, there is low variability within each a row. We'd guess that there is pretty good internal reliability here. Of course, the reliability coefficient, which summarizes the consistency here, is calculated in Question #30, and that will tell us if we are right. (We are.)

More questions? See #30, #31, and #32.

What Does Test-Retest Reliability Look Like?

In Question #18, we talked about different ways to show that a test is reliable. Each type of reliability centered on a different strategy for demonstrating consistency of scores. Test-retest reliability is interested in consistency across time.

Unlike validity, but like all types of reliability, a single value can be generated, which represents test-retest reliability. The reliability coefficient used in this case is the correlation between two sets of scores generated by the same group of people. See Question #28 for more details on correlations, but it is a number that indicates the strength of relationship (or consistency) between two sets of scores. Correlations range from −1.0 to +1.0, with values close to 0 meaning no relationship between the scores. So, for test-retest reliability evidence, a test developer or researcher gives a representative group of test takers the test in question and collects their scores. Sometime later, the same group of people takes the exact same test, and their scores are lined up into two columns. Each individual produced two scores—a score for the first occasion and a score from the second occasion. That is why this sort of reliability is called test-retest reliability. Then a correlation coefficient is calculated between the two columns of numbers. If the correlation suggests good consistency between testing times, that is treated as evidence of reliability.

Of course, the actual level of the measured construct or trait of interest can change across time, so test-retest reliability is only interesting if one does *not* expect change. So, choosing the amount of time between testing occasions depends on the definition of the construct. If one believes one is measuring something that doesn't change very quickly such as some semipermanent trait (intelligence or political attitude, for example), one would expect high correlations between testing occasions with long periods of time separating them, maybe even years. For those characteristics that change frequently, such as what psychologists call *states*, like mood, shorter periods of time are chosen for test-retest reliability analysis, such as a day or less. Most test-retest reliability estimates reported in test manuals or research articles are 2 to 6 weeks. It all depends on how stable you think your construct is. In fact, test-retest reliability is sometimes referred to as stability, with the correlation coefficient, which is calculated between the two measurement occasions, sometimes called a *stability coefficient*.

The data below represent four students who took the same intelligence test twice with a year between administrations. It is set up for a test-retest reliability study.

Test-Retest Reliability Study

Student	Testing Occasion 1	Testing Occasion 2
D'Artagnan	95	92
Athos	100	106
Porthos	117	110
Aramis	124	120

The correlation between the two testing occasions for this data is .92, which indicates excellent test-retest reliability.

More questions? See #17 and #79.

What Does Inter-rater Reliability Look Like?

Reliability is concerned about the amount of random error in the scores produced by a test. The source or "cause" of that random error can be in the test directions, the format of the items, the wording of the items, or the testing conditions, or there can be randomness in how the test is scored. The inconsistent application of scoring rules can affect *inter-rater reliability*.

We aren't talking about objectively scored tests here. By *randomness in scoring* we don't mean that a teacher and student can't come to terms on whether *B* or *C* is the correct answer on a disputed multiple-choice question. Randomness in scoring occurs when the scoring rules are subjective. A teacher or someone has to evaluate the quality of an answer or product and decide whether it gets 3 points or 2 points or 2½. When human judgment comes into play, that's when inter-rater reliability is a concern.

Studies to evaluate inter-rater reliability typically have a pair of "raters" who have both scored the same tests (or the same question on multiple tests). The hope is to establish that any single trained person can assign scores, so two scorers are used for the study to see if there is much subjectivity. How one assesses inter-rater reliability and analyzes the data, however, depends on the reasons for the testing. If the scores are to be used to make high-stakes decisions about individuals, there should be mostly perfect matches between scores. The *percentage of agreement*, or the percentage of times the two raters agreed, is an estimator for reliability in this situation. If the assessment is for research purposes and groups will be compared, the *correlation* between the pair of raters is all that matters (see Question #28). One judge might consistently score people higher than the other judge, but if their relative rankings are the same, then that allows for the necessary statistical analysis between different groups of people.

Imagine a study looking at the inter-rater reliability for a measure of writing ability. Students write short essays that are judged by trained experts and assigned a score of 0, 1, 2, or 3, following some established scoring procedures (such as a rubric; see Question #78). Here is the data from an inter-rater reliability study (much smaller, of course, than a real study would be):

	Judge A	*Judge B*	*Agreement?*
Essay 1	2	2	Yes
Essay 2	2	1	No
Essay 3	1	1	Yes
Essay 4	3	2	No
Essay 5	1	0	No

If the purpose of the essay test is to assign a score to an individual (such as a student), which is meant to represent his or her writing ability, and some judgment will be made about that *individual,* then we might conclude that the scoring rules for this test have low inter-rater reliability. The two judges, applying the same rules, only agreed 40% of the time.

If the purpose of the essay test is to measure change in a group of students before and after a unit on writing skills, then this data reflects decent inter-rater reliability for the scoring procedures. The correlation between the two judges' sets of scores is .79.

We know that a test might be valid for one purpose but not another (see Question #8). Here we discover that a test might be reliable for one purpose, but not another.

There are a couple of other, somewhat more sophisticated, methods of calculating inter-rater reliability that are more useful for certain research methodologies, such as *content analysis.* Cohen's *kappa* is often the preferred method for assessing inter-rater agreement when judges are asked to place items into categories. It works better than a simple percent agreement approach because there is certain to be some agreement just because of chance. After all, if there are only three categories of ratings in which to place an item, chance alone would expect two raters to agree 33% of the time. Cohen's kappa controls for that element of chance and removes it from the estimate. The calculations take the simple percent agreement and express it as the proportion of nonchance agreement that was achieved by raters. As a proportion, it ranges from 0 (no agreement) to 1.0 (perfect agreement). Krippendorff's *alpha* coefficient (not to be confused with Cronbach's *alpha*; see Question #32) also takes chance into account, as *kappa* does, but allows for more than two judges in a single analysis and also takes sample size into account when analyzing chance expectations. The math required for this estimation requires a computer.

More questions? See #17, #32, and #78.

Other Than the Three Main Types of Reliability, Are There Others?

Q uestions #21, #22, and #23 presented three types of reliability, three ways to demonstrate that a test is producing consistent scores with very little random fluctuation. *Internal reliability* looks at consistency across the items within a test. *Test-retest reliability* looks at the correlation between two administrations of the same test. In the case of subjective scoring, it is *inter-rater reliability* that estimates how much agreement there is among different scorers. There is a fourth way of exploring reliability, but it is usually of interest only for large-scale test developers. That other approach to reliability is called **parallel forms reliability**.

Parallel forms reliability looks at consistency between two different forms or versions of the same test. High-stakes tests, such as college admissions tests and certification exams for various professions (e.g., lawyers, teachers, nurses), must have more than one version of their tests. The results matter so much that the content of these tests is highly coveted and might be shared among ne'er-do-wells and others who are willing to encourage cheating for personal gain or monetary profit. For security purposes, the exact items that appear on a test are kept as secret as possible. One way security is maintained is to have several different groups of items that make up different forms of the test. That way, if your friend is taking a law school admissions test on a Saturday morning in New York, he can't call you and tell you about the questions before you take the same form that afternoon in California. Because you won't get the same group of items as she did.

Test makers who have different forms of the same test use a definition of test that is a bit more abstract than a classroom teacher's definition. Developers of high-stakes standardized instruments write and archive hundreds of questions, only some of which are needed for any given test form. They think of this large pool of validated items as their "test." They sample from this pool to create any particular form of that test.

Using different test forms sounds risky. Anyone doing poorly on one version of a test might complain of unfairness. Those who use the test scores to make decisions, like college admissions offices, might be concerned that one form of a test is less valid than another. One way that test developers ensure that different forms of tests are similar enough to each other that it makes no difference is to demonstrate equivalency through parallel forms reliability. Two forms of the same test are given to one group and their scores are correlated. Like other forms of reliability, the correlation is treated as an estimate of consistency. Very high correlations are usually required to demonstrate parallel forms reliability. Other similarities in the behavior of scores from both tests are required by measurement folks, as well, such as variability and the distribution of random errors, but it is the basic relationship between scores that is most important. Would you have done better or worse on some other form of this test? You want the answer to be "It wouldn't have mattered; all the test forms are equivalent."

More questions? See #85.

How Are Reliability and Validity Related to Each Other?

Question #17 focused on how reliability and validity are different from each other, but you're not crazy if you see these two concepts as overlapping in important ways. Validity is the characteristic of a test score that does, in fact, accurately represent the intended construct. If a test measures the trait it is supposed to measure, it is valid, or, to be technically correct, it produces *scores* that are valid. Reliability is the characteristic of a test score that remains consistent when measuring the same person. If there is no randomness affecting a test's scores, it is a reliable test.

The scores for a group of people on any test will vary across individuals, of course. If all of that variability is because people actually vary on the "amount" of the measured construct they have, then the scores are reliable. On the other hand, if the scores vary as they should because of different actual levels of the trait the test is intended to measure, that sounds like a validity argument. One way reliability and validity are related to each other is that they both refer to the absence of measurement error. It is just that validity is concerned about systematic error, and reliability is concerned about random error.

Another key relationship between reliability and validity is that if a test is low in reliability it cannot, logically, be high in validity. If a test is valid (or, more accurately, is high in validity), the scores it produces measure the construct with great accuracy. If one person's level of a trait is 10% higher than his or her brother's, the person's score should be 10% higher than his or her brother's. We're simplifying things a bit here because, of course, different scales can be used for valid measurement and not all of them reflect differences with the precision of differences, but you get the idea. If some of the variability of differences between individual scores is unrelated to the actual level of the measured trait because of, for example, low reliability, then validity is impossible. It is often said of reliability and validity (at least by measurement folks) that a test may be reliable without being valid, but if it is valid, then it must be reliable. See Question #17 for a discussion about why that is true, but for this answer, you can see how in some ways reliability is a *type* of validity. One cannot establish validity for an instrument without first establishing reliability, but if a test is reliable, it still might or *might not* be valid. To show the logical relationship between reliability and validity, this table answers a key question:

"Is it possible to have test scores that reflect both these characteristics?"

	Valid	Not Valid
Reliable	Yes	Yes
Not Reliable	No	Yes

More questions? See #7 and #17.

Some Types of Reliability Evidence Must Be More Important for Some Types of Tests, but Not Important for Other Types of Tests. What's the General Strategy for Making an Argument for the Reliability of a Test?

Reliability refers to the extent to which a test produces scores for individuals that do not randomly fluctuate. Scores should be consistent. Different types of reliability evidence emphasize different types of consistency. In the same way that different forms of validity arguments make sense for different tests depending on their different purposes, different forms of reliability arguments are most important for tests depending on how they will be used.

Any type of reliability argument has some value for every type of test, but there are "must-have" reliability arguments associated with different types of tests. This table shows the three most common types of reliability evidence, how they are estimated quantitatively, and the types of tests for which they are most useful.

	Inter-rater Reliability (Correlation or Percentage)	*Test-retest Reliability (Correlation)*	*Internal Reliability (Coefficient Alpha)*
Subjectively scored tests (e.g., performance-based assessments, essay tests, auditions, job interviews, medical diagnoses)	X		
Measures of stable traits (e.g., intelligence tests, personality assessments, genetics)		X	
High-stakes tests from which important decisions will be made on the basis of a single score (e.g., SAT, ACT, psychological tests)			X

When the decision is subjective, it is important that as concrete and predictable a system of scoring as possible be used. Inter-rater reliability examines whether that's the case. Some scores stick with us for a long time because they are meant to assess something that doesn't change quickly or easily. Those scores should remain relatively unchanged as demonstrated though test-retest reliability estimates. Finally, when there is a decision that will affect someone's life, such as college admissions, placement in special education, or a conclusion that someone has a personality disorder, internal reliability information helps determine whether the many items on a measure combine to produce a single, precise score.

More questions? See #15 and #18.

I Need to Build a Test. How Can I Make Sure It Is Reliable?

There are two aspects of test development that help ensure reliability. Remember that reliability refers to the amount of random inconsistency in the scores produced. So, two strategies will help reduce that foolish inconsistency and increase reliability:

1. Use objective scoring rules.

2. Make the test long.

Much of the random unpredictability in the scores from a test is due to the extent to which any human judgment is involved. If a teacher has to read an essay answer and decide in some subjective way whether the answer is correct or wrong or, maybe, partially correct, that means answers of the same quality might sometimes receive different judgments. The same answer in the morning might receive 3 points and in the afternoon receive 4 points. A teacher in a good mood might classify a reply as right, while a teacher following the same scoring rules might classify the reply as wrong. This is why high-stakes tests in education and in psychology almost always have very concrete, objective scoring criteria. Test takers deserve precise scores that don't vary unsystematically based on irrelevant factors, such as luck. Think of those dreaded multiple-choice finals in school. There's a good reason why they followed a dry objective scoring format ("Choose the one correct answer"). Say what you want about that type of test format, it is likely pretty reliable.

Another way to increase test reliability is to increase the number of observations. And test questions are observations. Picture that random fluctuation that affects a person's response to a test item. If I give many questions and add them all together to produce a single score, those random errors should cancel themselves out. This leaves a total score with very little random error in it. This is the main reason why those same high-stakes tests that have boring objective scoring rules are also very long. Many different questions are asked, and then they are summed into a single score representing *Verbal Ability* or *Algebra Skill* or *Attitude Toward These Kids Today* or your final course grade or whatever. This strategy is designed to increase reliability, not just to take up your whole Saturday morning.

So, decrease subjectivity in scoring and increase the number of components that go into a total score, and you've just used sophisticated scientific methods to improve the reliability of your test.

More questions? See #21, #22, and #23.

PART 4

THE STATISTICS OF MEASUREMENT

When Establishing Validity or Reliability, I Can Understand That Examining Whether Two Sets of Scores Are Related Is Important, but How Do I Do That?

There are two situations where the relationship between two sets of scores is interesting. First, researchers often wish to know whether two variables are related. For example, are anger and depression distinctive expressions of the same underlying emotion, or are they different? Knowing how strongly they are associated with each other would help to answer that question. The other situation where knowing the strength of the relationship between two variables is useful is in measurement. If scores on a new test should coincide with scores on some other similar test, and they *do*, that can become part of a validity argument for that new test. And if people score about the same on two different administrations of a test, that can become part of a reliability argument. The basic statistic in social science research used to assess the strength of the relationship between any two sets of scores is the **correlation coefficient**.

Correlation coefficients can only be computed with exactly two columns of scores that have been matched up—one group of people producing two sets of scores. They take into account the relative size of each score (how high or low it is within its own distribution), whether the paired scores are roughly equal in their relative standings (do they have the same rank order within their own distributions?), and the amount of variability in both score distributions. Relative standings and variability require first computing two key values in statistics, the **mean** and the **standard deviation**. A mean of a set of scores is the arithmetic average. One adds up all the values in a distribution and divides by the number of values. It provides a good summary of all the scores using just a single number. A standard deviation is the average distance of each score from the mean. A large standard deviation means that scores vary a lot, while a smaller standard deviation means scores are fairly close together. By taking into account both the mean and standard deviation in a distribution of scores, one can determine any given score's place in that distribution.

The full equation for computing a correlation coefficient is somewhat complex, but a simpler version of the equation exists, which uses a handy value called a Z. (Z's are described more completely in Question #87.) A Z compares each score with its mean and expresses the distance of that score from the mean in terms of standard deviations. Z's can be positive if a score is above the mean and negative if the score is below the mean. You'll notice that the correlation coefficient equation actually compares Z's to each other to find the relationship, not the raw scores themselves. Here is the formula for computing the relationship between two variables, let's say the scores from tests x and y:

$$\Sigma\ (\mathbf{ZxZy})\ /\ \textbf{Number of pairs of scores} - \textbf{1}$$

By multiplying the pairs of Z's by each other, adding up all those multiplications (the Σ means "add together"), and then dividing by the number of pairs, a correlation coefficient is produced.

Correlations range from −1 to +1, and the further from 0, the stronger the relationship between two sets of numbers. Whether a correlation is negative or positive depends only on how scores were assigned (do high scores mean a lot of whatever is measured or a little?) and do not indicate how strong the correlation is.

More questions? See #10 and #22.

How Can I Calculate a Number to See Whether a Test Has Content Validity?

*C*ontent validity is the characteristic of a test that includes a fair sampling of the questions that could or should be on the test. Arguments for content validity are usually based on referring to an accepted set of topics, abilities, or areas that ought to be covered for a test to measure whatever it is supposed to measure. This can be done by presenting some "official" or reasonable list of standards or content domains and demonstrating that items on the test represent those appropriately. One can also demonstrate content validity by asking experts to judge the representativeness of items on the test. There is a number that can be computed to support this "ask-the-experts" strategy.

The *content validity ratio* estimates how well a single item belongs on a test. It was originally developed to make decisions about whether particular questions belonged on job aptitude tests. Would someone who is good at his job need to know how to do this? The method can be used for any type of measure, however, to demonstrate content validity.

One assembles a group of judges who are experts in the content area to be assessed. Each judge rates each item as being "essential," "of some importance," or "unrelated to the topic." The key rating is whether an item is judged to be "essential." Data is gathered for all items from all judges, and then this formula is used to produce a content validity ratio:

$$\text{Content Validity Ratio} = \frac{N_{\text{essential}} - N/2}{N/2}$$

N is the total number of judges, and $N_{\text{essential}}$ is the number of judges who categorize an item as essential. The equation is more complicated than you might think it should be because we want to control for any chance or sloppy randomness when the experts categorize.

If you are living alone on a deserted island or for some other reason can't gather a group of experts, you can make your own ratings for each question on a test you develop and run the numbers yourself. A good content validity ratio for an item is anything over 0, with ratios close to 1 indicating particularly essential questions.

More questions? See #8 and #9.

For Reliability's Sake, I Can See That Showing a Test Is Consistent Within Itself Is Important, but How Do I Do That?

To demonstrate that responses to individual items within a test are not random, one strategy for showing reliability is to show constancy in responses across items. On an attitude scale, is your answer on Question 1 similar to your answer on Question 4? On that state math test, if you got Question 1 correct, did you also get Question 4 correct? A traditional method for exploring internal reliability is to cut a test in half and correlate the halves together. This type of reliability evidence is, understandably, called **split-half reliability**.

Let's explore the data from an imaginary four-item attitude survey. All the questions are meant to ask about attitude toward the color blue, and all responses will be summed together into a single total score representing *attitude toward blue*. Consequently, it would be appropriate to establish that all the items measure the same thing and are internally consistent.

Respondent	Item 1	Item 2	Item 3	Item 4	Total Score
Washington	4	4	5	2	15
Adams	1	3	1	1	6
Jefferson	3	2	4	2	11

Assume that responses are scaled so that a 5 means a positive feeling toward blue and a 1 means a negative feeling. (For reliability analyses, you don't even need to know what the questions actually ask. See how different that is from a validity analysis?) By looking at the total scores, you can see that there is great variability in attitude within the group, but that isn't what reliability cares about. Reliability is concerned with the variability within each single person's responses across items within the test.

To compute split-half reliability, we first take everyone's score and turn it into two scores—one for each half of the test. One can split a test into any number of "halves," and they don't even have to be equal in number of items for the math to work. For this example, we will take the first two items (1 and 2) for everyone and sum those for a score on one half and sum the other two items (3 and 4) for our scores on the other half. That would produce a pair of scores for all our participants:

Participant	Score on 1st Half	Score on 2nd Half
Washington	8	7
Adams	4	2
Jefferson	5	6

Using this data, we would compute a correlation coefficient (see Question #28 for the formula for the correlation coefficient). The correlation is .82, so our split-half reliability estimate for this *attitude toward blue* measure is .82. As a rule of thumb, internal reliabilities above .70 are good, so a reliability estimate of .82 would be very good. By the way, Question #31 shows how this split-half reliability estimate actually underestimates reliability and can be improved, so be sure to check it out for more information about this simple and quick method of estimating internal consistency.

More questions? See #18 and #21.

How Can I Improve the Accuracy of the Split-Half Reliability Coefficient?

In Question #30, we talked about split-half reliability, a traditional, and fairly simple, way to calculate internal consistency for a group of items. By correlating scores from two halves of a test, one can estimate the proportion of variability among scores that is true score variance and not just random fluctuation (see Question #17). Though it makes sense on its face that split-half reliability is a way of determining internal reliability, there is a problem with the method. It turns out that this method will underestimate reliability. Fortunately, we can figure out the amount of underestimation and correct for it. The tool that does this for us is the **Spearman-Brown Prophecy Formula**.

This formula is named after two different researchers who suggested the same solution at about the same time. They both realized that the problem with a straightforward split-half correlation as an estimate for reliability is that it is not calculating the correlation of a test with itself (the definition of reliability); it's calculating the correlation of a test with a version of itself that is only half as long! One mathematical truth about reliability is that longer tests, those made up of more items, are more reliable. So, a fairer, more accurate, reliability estimate for the actual test at its full length would take this fact into account. That's what the Spearman-Brown Prophecy Formula does. As the name, suggests, it *predicts* what that split-half correlation would be for a test twice as long. Here is the equation:

**New Split-Half Reliability = 2 (Old Split-Half Correlation) /
1 + Old Split-Half Correlation**

Unless you start with perfect reliability, this will always result in a new estimate that is larger than the original. Let's try it with a variety of split-half reliability estimates:

Original Split-Half Reliability	Calculations	Predicted Split-Half Reliability
.50	1.0 / 1.50	.67
.70	1.40 / 1.70	.82
.90	1.80 / 1.90	.95

This formula is sometimes called the *Step-Up Formula* because the original estimate for split-half reliability always increases a bit. You might notice that the higher the reliability starts, the less it will increase.

There is an assumption that any increase in test length would be with items that are similar to those on the existing scale in terms of their correlation with each other. In the real world, this is hard to guarantee, so the Spearman-Brown Prophecy Formula just acts as a guide as to whether it is worth it to add items.

The formula for adjusting split-half reliability is a special case of a more general formula that can predict reliability for a new version of a test that is changed proportionately in any number of ways. It doesn't have to be twice its original length. It can even be shorter. The full formula uses a proportional adjustment of new length to old length (which is 2 / 1, or 2 in our case) and looks like this:

$$\frac{\left(\dfrac{\textbf{New Length}}{\textbf{Old Length}}\right) \times \textbf{Old Split - Half Correlation}}{1 + \left(\dfrac{\textbf{New Length}}{\textbf{Old Length}} - 1\right) \times \textbf{Old Split - Half Correlation}}$$

More questions? See #21 and #30.

I Never See Split-Half Reliability Reported. Is There a More Common Way to Show That a Test Has Internal Consistency?

There has been another formula for calculating an internal reliability estimate for decades, but it is only fairly recently that this has become the preferred way to report reliability for a test. This is likely because the math is fairly complex. At least, it is much more complicated than just correlating two halves of a test and requires computers (or handheld calculators) to quickly compute. This modern estimate is **coefficient alpha**, or *Cronbach's alpha*, named after the educational psychologist who invented it in 1951.

Coefficient alpha is determined using a formula that takes into account the length of a test (which we know affects reliability) and the strength of correlations among the items on the test (which we know also affects reliability). Essentially, coefficient alpha calculates the proportion of test score variance that is not random, but reflects actual true score variance (see Question #17).

You'll likely never have to work it by hand, but here is the formula for coefficient alpha:

(Number of items/Number of items – 1) ×
(1 – [Sum of item variances/Variance of total score])

The top portion of the formula reflects the length of a test; the larger this value, the larger the coefficient alpha will be. The bottom portion of the formula estimates similarities on scores across items. A larger value here will also result in a larger alpha.

Alpha ranges from 0.0 to 1.0. It can be lower than 0.0, but this is rarely the case with real and correctly entered data. The customary interpretations of coefficient alpha in terms of whether a test's reliability is "good enough" are whether the test is used for group research purposes, in which case it can be comparatively low (.60 or higher), or will be used for making high-stakes decisions about individuals, which requires highly reliable measures (alphas above .90). Common guidelines for interpreting coefficient alpha are

Coefficient alpha	Interpretation
Below .60	Unacceptable
.60–.69	Acceptable
.70–.79	Good
.80–.89	Very Good
.90 and above	Excellent

More questions? See #30 and #31.

We've Got Two Ways to Establish Internal Reliability. Which Way Is Best?

We have presented in earlier questions two different ways to calculate a number that estimates internal consistency for a test. Both are based on the correlations among items within the test. *Split-half reliability* is the correlation between scores from two different halves of the same test. *Coefficient alpha* takes a more complex approach and determines the proportion of total score variance, which is true score variance and not random variability in responses. Too much information can be a dangerous thing, and having two different options presents a dilemma. Which method should we use? Though split-half reliability is easier to calculate, almost every test developer, educational researcher, and test manual reports coefficient alpha as the estimate of internal reliability. That's because there is a big limitation to the split-half correlation approach.

A given test can be divided into any number of "halves." The split-half correlation procedure can compute a correlation between any of those possible pairs of halves. The halves don't even have to be the same length (include the same number of items) for the procedure to produce a correlation. So, imagine a 10-item test. You could create your two halves by using the odd numbered items for one half and the even numbered items for the other half. That would be perfectly reasonable. Or you could take Items 1 to 5 for the first half and Items 6 to 10 for the second half. That also would be reasonable. So, which is best? Both make sense and, in fact, there are dozens of other ways you could get your halves. You could take items 1, 2, 7, and 9 for a half and items 3, 4, 5, 6, 8, and 10 for the other. Get the idea? The problem is that it matters which way you split a test. You will get slightly different correlations with any of the different approaches.

Using the attitude survey data from Question #30, let's split a test into several different possible halves to demonstrate how the split-half correlation will vary:

Respondent	Item 1	Item 2	Item 3	Item 4	Total Score
Washington	4	4	5	2	15
Adams	1	3	1	1	6
Jefferson	3	2	4	2	11

Items in Half A	Items in Half B	Test Takers	Score A	Score B	Split-Half Correlation
1 and 2	3 and 4	Washington	8	7	.82
		Adams	4	2	
		Jefferson	5	6	
1 and 3	2 and 4	Washington	9	6	.72
		Adams	2	4	
		Jefferson	7	4	
1 and 4	2 and 3	Washington	6	9	.92
		Adams	2	4	
		Jefferson	5	6	
1	2, 3, and 4	Washington	4	11	.98
		Adams	1	5	
		Jefferson	3	8	

The different split-half correlations range from .72 to .98. They can't all be the best estimate of reliability and maybe none of them are. The most accurate estimate, the fairest thing to do, theoretically, would be to calculate all the possible split-half correlations (correct them with the Spearman-Brown Prophecy Formula; see Question #31) and then average all those possible split-half reliability estimates. That average would be your best estimate of reliability for a test. Well, that's what coefficient alpha does. Coefficient alpha reliability for a test is the average of all the possible split-half reliabilities. That's why it's the preferred internal reliability estimate.

More questions? See #30, #31, and #32.

How Can I Use Reliability Coefficients to Improve My Validity Estimates?

W e discussed in Question #25 how reliability and validity are conceptually related. Without reliability, a test cannot have validity. This theoretical relationship manifests itself in a very real mathematical relationship, as well.

A common strategy for evaluating whether a test measures what it is supposed to measure is to correlate it with scores from some other test. For instance, if the developers of the brand-new *Rohlf Intelligence Test* want people to trust that it really measures intelligence as well as the more highly regarded *Wechsler Intelligence Scale for Children*, they might conduct a study where they give both tests to the same group of students. The correlation between the two sets of scores would be treated as a quantitative summary of the validity of the Rohlf test. A high correlation would demonstrate validity, while a low correlation would be difficult to explain from a marketing perspective. The size of that "validity coefficient," however, is limited statistically by the reliability of both tests.

It makes sense that low reliability would lessen the size of possible correlations between two sets of scores because reliability is an indication of the amount of randomness in a set of scores. Random numbers are unlikely to correlate with each other, so two sets of scores that are substantially random will not correlate highly. There exists a mathematical formula that capitalizes on what is known about this relationship between reliability and correlations to estimate what the correlation would be (or, technically, *might* be) between two measures if they had perfect reliability. The question is, If these two sets of scores that have some randomness in them can still produce a correlation *this* big, how big might the *true* relationship be between the underlying constructs if the measurement could be done without random error? The *correction for attenuation* formula estimates an answer to that intriguing question.

Here is the correction for attenuation equation:

$$\text{Corrected Correlation} = \frac{\textbf{Observed Correlation}}{\sqrt{(\textbf{Reliability}_1 \times \textbf{Reliability}_2)}}$$

Procedurally, you take the two coefficient alphas for the two tests, multiply them together, and take the square root of that product. Then, you divide the actual correlation you've found by that quantity. This will result in a higher correlation, which should be interpreted as the possible strength of the theoretical relationship between the two constructs meant to be measured by the two tests. It should not be treated as the true correlation between the two *tests*, of course, because you've already calculated that, and reality can't be changed.

Here are some examples of how correction for attenuation produces estimates of theoretical relationships from observed correlations:

Observed Correlation	Test 1 Reliability	Test 2 Reliability	Theoretical Correlation
.50	.80	.85	.61
.50	.60	.65	.81
.40	.80	.85	.49
.40	.60	.65	.65

More questions? See #8 and #17.

What Useful Information Can I Get by Analyzing Individual Items on a Test?

While tests are being developed and even after they are done, test makers continuously seek to revise and improve their instruments. In addition to collecting and evaluating validity and reliability evidence, information about individual items or tasks is useful for determining if they belong on the test. Do they help validity? Do they help reliability? Do they function as they should?

Especially for achievement tests, there are three basic *questions about questions* that can be answered through simple statistical analyses. Data about responses to individual items can tell us what students know, which questions are key to distinguishing between those who have a lot of knowledge and those who have less knowledge, and what errors in understanding students have.

By simply looking at the proportion of test takers who got a question correct, we can determine **item difficulty**. This handy statistic is explored in Question #36.

By looking at the relationship between performance on the total test and performance on a single item, we can make a judgment about whether a question measures what the test as a whole measures. **Item discrimination** is covered in Question #37.

A third common type of item analysis especially valuable for classroom teachers using multiple-choice tests is to examine an item in terms of which answer options were chosen. How many got the question right, and, for those who missed it, which wrong answer option did they choose? This procedure is called **distractor analysis** because the wrong answer options on a multiple-choice question are referred to as distractors.

Distractor analysis works this way. Imagine this multiple-choice question from a classroom quiz over a classic Mark Twain novel:

In *Adventures of Huckleberry Finn,* who is Huck's traveling companion when he journeys down the Mississippi River on a raft?

A. Jim

B. Pap

C. Tom

D. Aunt Polly

Imagine that 63% of the students in this class got the question correct. The right answer is *A. Jim,* and it is likely that if students read most of the book, that would be an obviously correct answer. We know that about a third of students missed the question, but the teacher doesn't know if one of the wrong answers was commonly chosen, indicating that there is a frequent error in understanding or memory among those who missed the item, or whether there was just blind guessing going on (suggesting that the book was unread by many). A distractor analysis would count the number of students who chose each option and display the results as percentages. Consider this distractor analysis for this item:

Answer Option	Percentage Choosing Option
*A	63%
B	12%
C	14%
D	11%

* The keyed (or correct) answer.

The wrong answer choices of B, C, and D seem fairly equally popular. This suggests that those who didn't know the correct answer just picked an answer randomly.

Teachers can use this distractor analysis technique to identify any common misunderstandings or errors in thinking. They can also check to see if a distractor is working. If no one ever picks a given answer option, it is not really functioning as a plausible possibility, and teachers can rewrite the question for future reuse.

More questions? See #73 and #77.

How Do I Calculate and Interpret the Difficulty of a Test Question?

One way of finding out whether a group of people, like students in a class-room, knows something (e.g., a fact, a concept, information) is to analyze a single question that asks about that knowledge domain and see how difficult it was. How many people knew the right answer? If many people knew the answer, then, by definition, the question was easy. If many people did not know the answer, then the question was hard. A simple equation is used to determine *item difficulty*:

$$\text{Item Difficulty} = \frac{\textbf{Number of People Who Got the Question Right}}{\textbf{Total Number of People Who Took the Test}}$$

So, the common way to compute item difficulty is to divide the number of correct answers by the number of all answers (whether wrong or right). This finds the proportion of people who chose the correct answer. As a proportion, this *difficulty index* ranges from 0 to 1.0. Values close to 1.0 indicate easy questions; values close to 0 indicate difficult questions.

This formula works very well for objectively scored questions and tasks, like multiple-choice items, because the possible "scores" on these sorts of items are usually 0 (for a miss) and 1 (for a correct response), but the difficulty index can be calculated for items with a wider range of possible points, too. The more general procedure for item difficulty requires scoring each item as "what proportion of possible points did the individual get?" So, if the points possible for, say, an essay question range from 0 to 5, a student's score of 3 becomes 3/5, or .67. Then, all those individual scores on a single question are averaged. That average is the item difficulty. The first equation shown is so simple because for "wrong or right = 0 or 1" items like multiple-choice questions, the math works out to the same result.

The right way to interpret a difficulty index depends on the purpose of the item. Imagine a difficulty index for a particular question of .90. If a classroom teacher is interpreting this value for a question on one of his tests, he might be pleased. After all, clearly most everyone has learned this fact or mastered this concept. His teaching has been successful and an instructional objective has been met. Developers of standardized, norm-referenced tests, though, may be concerned by a difficulty index that is so high. If the purpose of their test is to distinguish between those who know a lot and those who know less, an item this easy is not particularly helpful. If everyone gets it right, the question is not helpful in distinguishing among a wide range of people with a wide range of ability levels. A question with a difficulty index of .90 might be removed from future revisions of the test.

More questions? See #73 and #77.

What Is Item Discrimination, and How Do I Calculate It?

W hen a test is supposed to measure knowledge or skill, like most of the tests you take in school, each question or item by itself should measure that knowledge or skill. Each item should measure the same thing as the total test itself. The item discrimination index is a way of calculating how well an individual question does that. How well does an item "discriminate" between high scorers and low scorers on the test? The idea is that if there is no relationship between how people perform on a single question and the total score on the test, then that item probably doesn't belong on the test.

There are two ways to compute a discrimination index for an item. The first is to calculate the correlation between the item and the total test. Items are usually scored by assigning a 1 if test takers got the answer right and a 0 if they missed it. For example, imagine this data for four students who took a state math test:

Student	Score on Question #17	Total Score on the Test
Groucho	1	120
Chico	1	105
Harpo	1	95
Gummo	0	80

The correlation between the two columns of scores is .79. This is a very high discrimination index and suggests that Item 17 belongs on this test. Generally, any value over 0 is acceptable for a discrimination index (though many commercial testing companies want them to be much higher).

A simpler way to compute an approximate discrimination index (at least, a method that doesn't require a computer for the calculations) is frequently used by real-life schoolteachers who want to analyze their own test questions. This entails dividing the test into two groups—the high scorers on the total test and the low scorers—and comparing the two groups in terms of the difficulty for that item. One would expect that more people in the high-scoring group would get a question correct than in the low-scoring group. For the data shown, if we divide the class so that Groucho and Chico are in the high-scoring group (above 100) and

Harpo and Gummo are in the low-scoring group (below 100), we see that the difficulty for the high scorers was 1.0 (the proportion of people getting it right; you might recognize this as the difficulty index from Question #36) and for the low scorers was .50 (half of the group got it right). To estimate a discrimination index, you subtract the low scorers' value from the value for the high scorers: 1.0 − .50 = .50. The approximate discrimination index from this method for Item 17 is .50. This suggests the same interpretation as the correlational method. Item #17 seems to measure whatever the whole test measures. It belongs.

More questions? See #35, #36, and #77.

What Is the Relationship Between Item Difficulty and Item Discrimination?

Item difficulty, as explained in Question #36, is computed as the proportion of test takers who got the correct answer on an exam question. As a proportion, it can range from 0 to 1.0, with values closer to 1.0 indicating an easy question that most people got right. Discrimination, discussed in Question #37, is how well a single item discriminates between those scoring high and those scoring low on the whole test. It ranges from −1.0 to +1.0, with values above 0 indicating that those who did well on the entire test were more likely to get the question right. Values less than 0 mean that, for some reason, high scorers did less well on that item than low scorers.

The two indices represent different characteristics of questions. The discrimination index can be thought of as an indicator of validity because if a question is related to the total test score, it likely measures the same thing, to some extent, as the total test. Likewise, while a difficulty index isn't a direct indicator of the reliability of a question, certain item difficulty values lend themselves to producing tests with good internal consistency. A test full of items with .50 difficulties theoretically produces an achievement test with the highest possible internal reliability.

There are some mathematical relationships between difficulty and discrimination indices. This is a result of how the two values are calculated. Imagine an item with a difficulty index of 0.0. That means that there were literally no test takers who got the item correct. If that's the case, then the same number of high scorers got the question right (none) as did the low scorers (also none). That will result in a discrimination index of 0. So, if difficulty is too low, the discrimination index cannot, mathematically, be very good. The same is true for an item that is too easy. If everyone knows the answer to a question, it cannot possibly discriminate between the high-scoring group and the low-scoring group. That sort of item also has a discrimination index of 0. The relationship works the other way, as well. Certain discrimination indices require certain difficulty indices. Imagine a perfectly discriminating item. The top half of all test takers got the question correct, while the bottom half missed the question. That, by definition, means that 50% of folks got an item correct. That results in a difficulty index of .50 every time. So, there is a *sort* of relationship between difficulty and discrimination. Discrimination is limited the further an item's difficulty index is from .50, and difficulty indices move toward .50 when items discriminate well.

More questions? See #35 and #77.

PART 5

ACHIEVEMENT TESTS

What Are Achievement Tests, and How Are They Used?

An achievement test is a test of knowledge. Sometimes tests that are primarily achievement tests also measure skill or ability (such as writing skill, computational ability, or reading comprehension), but they almost always measure "school stuff." So, a teacher-made history quiz over World War II and that standardized statewide science test required for all eleventh graders in your district are both examples of achievement tests. Though there are many types of item formats that can appear on an achievement test, traditionally these tests, whether administered on a computer or on paper, consist of many, many multiple-choice questions.

As the name implies, achievement tests are designed to measure the current state of achievement. What does a student know today, right now? This distinguishes achievement tests from aptitude tests, which are meant to predict future performance, or personality instruments used to describe the psychological characteristics and traits of individuals. Though not labeled as such, some achievement tests such as the SAT, ACT, and GRE are actually used as aptitude tests and are used to predict future college performance.

Of the several types of validity evidence and arguments that can come to bear to judge the quality of an achievement test, it is *content validity* that plays the central role (see Question #9). Typically, items are written to adequately cover an agreed-upon set of standards, domains, skills, or topics, and a demonstration of that fact largely establishes validity.

Achievement tests, especially the large-scale statewide variety mandated by recent federal legislation, have become more common than ever, and much of a teacher's instructional time is now taken up with preparing for achievement tests, administering predictive tests of how their students will do on the state tests, administering the state tests themselves, and interpreting and responding to the results of state tests. There is even a movement in many places to use achievement test scores not only as a measure of student achievement, or *proficiency*, but also as a measure of a teacher's ability. Consequently, the achievement test is a central focus of educational measurement.

More questions? See #42, #43, and #44.

How Is the Validity of an Achievement Test Established?

Like developers of any assessment, developers of achievement tests draw from the broad menu of types of validity evidence when arguing that their tests are measuring what they are supposed to. They might demonstrate that their tests have *content validity* by showing that the questions themselves are a fair representation of all the questions that should be on the test. They could argue that scores on their tests correlate with other indicators of achievement and make a claim of *criterion validity*. In addition to these two common approaches, sometimes those who produce achievement tests refer to the nature of the underlying abilities or skills that they claim to measure and make a statement of *construct validity*.

A content validity argument for achievement tests is exemplified by frequent reports produced by those who make the *ACT* test. Their content validity claim is that the items on their tests closely align with school curricula. They routinely review state educational standards, survey educators, and consult with content area experts to identify what students should be expected to know.

Because many achievement tests are used for college admissions and are meant to predict college performance, criterion validity arguments are standard for these tests. The *SAT*, for example, in a 2008 report, showed that scores on each of their three test sections correlated moderately (see Question #28) with the grade point average of college freshmen:

	Correlation With Grade Point Average at End of Freshman Year
Critical Reading	.29
Mathematics	.26
Writing	.33

Though our definition of achievement tests suggests that these measures primarily assess knowledge, most college admissions tests include some measure of ability. The ability to think critically or write analytically, for example, is a common construct meant to be measured by many of these tests. The developers of the *GRE*, for example, argue that their test scores have construct validity because they measure the important skills for success in graduate school. They identify those skills as verbal ability, critical thought, and quantitative reasoning and claim to assess how well test takers demonstrate this type of thinking so necessary for graduate school completion.

More questions? See #8 and #9.

How Is the Reliability of an Achievement Test Established?

The common achievement tests, such as the *SAT* and the *ACT*, typically use one of two formats for their items. Most of the tests are made up of many (sometimes hundreds of) multiple-choice questions. Additionally, achievement tests, such as the *ACT* and *SAT*, often include an open-ended essay question. The nature of the scoring differs between these two formats, as does the type of reliability argument, which must be made in order to trust that the scores produced are precise, consistent, and not random.

The key reliability concern for groups of objectively scored items, like the computer scored multiple-choice questions on achievement tests, is that they all somehow represent a single broad topic or subject. After all, why add all the items together to compute a single score, unless they all measure the same thing? The type of reliability that is concerned with consistency of responses within a group of similar questions is *internal reliability*. Internal reliability is typically calculated statistically by looking at the correlations among all the relevant items and producing a value, *coefficient alpha*. Coefficient alpha is a proportion that (almost always) ranges from 0 to 1.0. The closer to 1.0, the more reliable the group of items. Very high internal reliability values (above .9) are usually expected from tests for which important decisions on individuals are made. Such high coefficient alphas are possible, though, especially when a test consists of many items. This is one reason why there are so many questions on achievement tests and one reason why achievement tests tend to produce internal reliability estimates above .9 for any given topic area or subtest.

The main reliability problem with human-scored essay questions is that there is so much judgment involved. The subjective nature of the ratings assigned by even well-trained scorers (such as those used by the SAT and ACT folks) makes consistency difficult. The SAT, for example, uses six different ratings or categories of quality and describes those categories in concrete ways with multiple criteria (e.g., "Exhibits skillful use of language, using a varied, accurate and apt vocabulary"). They also use high school and college English teachers as their raters and train them until they show great consistency with other experienced raters. Finally, two independent different raters are used for each essay, and their scores are combined to further increase precision. This type of reliability, which reflects agreement among human beings, is called *inter-rater reliability*. It can be represented with a percentage (what percent of the time did any two raters agree on the exact score to assign?), with a correlation between two raters scoring the same stack of essays, or by simply reporting the average distance between the scores assigned by different judges.

More questions? See #17 and #18.

What Does SAT Stand for, and What's the Test All About?

The *SAT* is an achievement test overseen by The College Board, a nonprofit association of colleges, designed to measure the kinds of skills useful in college—reading, writing, and math. It is administered and analyzed by Educational Testing Service, another nonprofit organization, which is responsible for a bunch of tests such as the GRE graduate school admissions test and Advanced Placement high school tests. The letters *S*, *A*, and *T* officially stand for nothing these days, though in the past, they were an abbreviation for *Scholastic Aptitude Test.* The term *aptitude* referred to its use as a predictive measure for how one would perform in college courses, but the word has sometimes become synonymous with *ability* or *intelligence,* and the SAT was never meant to measure those sorts of traits.

High school students take the SAT in order to prepare for college admission, and many colleges require SAT scores (or the scores of other admissions tests such as the *ACT*) as part of their applications. There are actually three tests that make up the SAT. They are *Critical Reading, Writing,* and *Mathematics,* and it takes a little under 4 hours total to complete all three. Scores on each test range from 200 to 800, with average scores of 500 and standard deviations of 100. A "total" score for the SAT is reported, and it is the three test scores added together. So, there is a range of 600 to 2400 possible on the SAT.

The SAT is typically used to give colleges some idea of which potential students will do well, and the test does an ok, but not great, job at that. Correlations between the SAT total score and performance in the first year of college (e.g., grade point average at the end of the first year) tend to be around .40, and correlations between scores on the three individual tests and relevant courses (such as between the *SAT Math* test and a college math class) are about the same. Statisticians would consider these correlations to be between small and moderate, but colleges continue to rely on these sorts of tests because they, at least, provide some information on which to make decisions.

The SAT includes an essay section, but it is mostly full of multiple-choice questions. Here is an example (provided by *The College Board*) of what a typical SAT test question looks like:

Choose the word or set of words that, when inserted in the sentence, best fits the meaning of the sentence as a whole.

Many forests in the southern region of the continent are _____ plant and animal diversity, partly because they never suffered the onslaught of glaciers that wiped out flora and fauna in northern forests long ago.

A. *rich in*

B. *devoid of*

C. *dependent on*

D. *protected from*

E. *conflicted about*

(The correct answer is *A.*)

More questions? See #44 and #46.

That Other Big College Admissions Test, the ACT: What Is It, and How Does It Differ From the SAT?

Like the SAT, the initials *ACT* no longer officially stand for anything, but it is the complete name for the test formerly known as the *American College Test.* Produced by a nonprofit organization of the same name, ACT, Inc., the test shares a similar purpose with the SAT. The ACT is meant to measure high school students' achievement and their ability to succeed in college courses.

Four areas are covered by the assessment, and four separate scores are produced: *English, Mathematics, Reading,* and *Science.* There is also an optional Writing test, which requires writing an original essay. *English* is defined here as "standard written English and rhetorical skills" and is distinct from *Reading,* which is focused on reading comprehension. The *Science* test, which is not a topic on the SAT, refers to the analytic and problem-solving skills that are commonly required for success in the natural sciences.

Scores on each of the four ACT tests range from 1 to 36, with a total composite score across all four tests created by averaging the individual scores. ACT reports that these scores in the four areas indicate readiness for college: English, 18; Math, 22; Reading, 21; Science, 24. Average scores on the ACT tend to be around 20 with a standard deviation of about 4½.

Here's what a typical item (provided by ACT, Inc.) looks like:

A car averages 27 miles per gallon. If gas costs $4.04 per gallon, which of the following is closest to how much the gas would cost for this car to travel 2,727 typical miles?

A. *$44.44*

B. *$109.08*

C. *$118.80*

D. *$408.04*

E. *$444.40*

(The correct answer is *D.*)

The ACT differs from the SAT in several important ways. First, the coverage of subjects is somewhat different. Second, the ACT essay requirement is optional, while the SAT essay portion is a required part of that assessment. Third, the scoring works differently in a way that might affect your strategy for doing well on the test. On the SAT, one is penalized for attempting and missing a question. This means that in addition to not getting any credit for the question, you actually lose points for guessing wrong. On the ACT, you can guess all you'd like and no harm will come to you. Among other test-taking tactics, if you are running out of time on the ACT, you should quickly choose an answer, even a random answer, on all the remaining items. On the SAT, you'd be better off leaving questions unanswered if you would just be guessing blindly.

More questions? See #42 and #44.

For Admission to Graduate School, My College Requires the GRE Test. What Is It, and Why Is It Better Than the SAT or ACT for Graduate School?

Like many other acronyms for college admissions tests, *GRE* used to stand for something, but the test is now only officially referred to by its initials. The test formerly known as the *Graduate Record Examination* is designed to measure verbal, quantitative, critical thinking, and analytical reasoning ability. It is used by most graduate schools in the United States to help make admission decisions.

The GRE's purpose is a bit different from those achievement tests meant for application to undergraduate programs because it is designed to assess those specific skills that are believed to be critical for success at the graduate and professional school level where the training is focused on advanced degrees such as masters' and doctorates. ETS, the organization that builds the GRE, believes the measured skills are closely aligned to the type of thinking that graduate students do and are not specific to any particular field of study or career.

The most recent version of the *GRE*, the *Revised General Test*, has three sections:

- **Verbal Reasoning**

  A multiple-choice test that assesses your ability to analyze sentences, recognize relationships among words, and evaluate written material.

- **Quantitative Reasoning**

  Focuses on math skills and the ability to analyze and understand data.

- **Analytical Writing**

  You are asked to write an essay so your ability to present and support complex ideas can be evaluated.

By looking at this list of the three sections and the nature of the questions and tasks, we can infer that, apparently, the difference between success in undergraduate and graduate school is believed to be one's competency in verbal skills, critical thought, and quantitative reasoning.

A fairly new scoring system is used on the GRE. Ever since 2011, on the multiple-choice sections, standardized scores range from 130 to 170, with all the whole values in between as possible scores. The mean is around 151 with a standard deviation of about 7½. For the analytical writing test, ratings are assigned from 0 to 6, using ½-point increments, with a mean of about 3.7 and a standard deviation just under 1.

Here's what a typical GRE item looks like:

Since 1813 reaction to Jane Austen's novels has oscillated between _____ and condescension; but in general later writers have esteemed her works more highly than did most of her literary _____.

A. *dismissal; admirers*

B. *adoration; contemporaries*

C. *disapproval; readers*

D. *indifference; followers*

E. *approbation; precursors*

(The correct answer is *B.*)

More questions? See #42, #43, and #45.

What Are the Major Tests for Professional Schools, and What Are They Like?

While generalized achievement tests exist and are commonly required for admission to college, certain professional fields require specialized tests that are designed to assess the knowledge base and skill areas necessary for success in their training programs. Three common professional school tests used in this way are the *Graduate Management Admissions Test* (GMAT), used for business schools, the *Medical College Admission Test* (MCAT), and the *Law School Admission Test* (LSAT).

The *GMAT*'s structure is similar to that of the *GRE* (see Question #44), but the questions themselves tend to be more relevant to the context of management and business. There are *Verbal* and *Quantitative* subtests, something called *Integrated Reasoning*, which involves data interpretation and analysis, and a written essay. The total standardized score on the GMAT ranges from 200 to 800 with a set mean of 500 and a standard deviation of 100. A sample item provided by the GMAT folks looks like this:

The cost of producing radios in Country Q is ten percent less than the cost of producing radios in Country Y. Even after transportation fees and tariff charges are added, it is still cheaper for a company to import radios from Country Q to Country Y than to produce radios in Country Y.

The statements above, if true, best support which of the following assertions?

A. *Labor costs in Country Q are ten percent below those in Country Y.*

B. *Importing radios from Country Q to Country Y will eliminate ten percent of the manufacturing jobs in Country Y.*

C. *The tariff on a radio imported from Country Q to Country Y is less than ten percent of the cost of manufacturing the radio in Country Y.*

D. *The fee for transporting a radio from Country Q to Country Y is more than ten percent of the cost of manufacturing the radio in Country Q.*

E. *It takes ten percent less time to manufacture a radio in Country Q than it does in Country Y.*

(The correct answer is *C.*)

The *MCAT* has three sections—two measuring mostly knowledge, *Physical Sciences* and *Biological Sciences*, and one measuring ability, *Verbal Reasoning*. Scores on each test range from 1 to 15. The total of all three test scores averages about 25 with a standard deviation of around 6½. Keeping in mind that most applicants to medical school have studied biology or "pre-med" in college, here is a sample MCAT item:

The nasal mucosa cells responsible for the release of excessive fluid during the common cold can best be classified as:

A. *epithelial*

B. *connective*

C. *contractile*

D. *neurosecretory*

(The correct answer is *A,* of course.)

The *LSAT* includes three sections (which are scored), all multiple-choice in format: *Reading Comprehension, Analytical Reasoning,* and *Logical Reasoning.* Scores are standardized for each section and for the total test, with means of about 151 and a standard deviation around 10. A typical LSAT item is as follows:

A century in certain ways is like a life, and as the end of a century approaches, people behave toward that century much as someone who is nearing the end of life does toward that life. So just as people in their last years spend much time looking back on the events of their life, people at a century's end _____ .
Which one of the following most logically completes the argument?

A. *reminisce about their own lives*

B. *fear that their own lives are about to end*

C. *focus on what the next century will bring*

D. *become very interested in the history of the century just ending*

E. *reflect on how certain unfortunate events of the century could have been avoided*

(The correct answer is *D.*)

More questions? See #39 and #40.

How Do I Score High on an Achievement Test?

Achievement tests are designed to measure knowledge. And achievement tests tend to be pretty reliable and valid. Consequently, the most effective way to score high on an achievement test is to have a lot of knowledge. Even with a high level of the construct of interest, however, test-taking ability can further affect your score. High anxiety can hurt performance, while strong preparation and application of good strategies can help.

There are a variety of things you can do to help you score as high as possible on a test like the *ACT, SAT,* or *GRE*:

- **Know what to expect.**
  - ○ Study online descriptions of the tests provided by the test makers. All the big tests have helpful Web sites that describe what the tests measure, what the subtests are, how answers are scored, and so on. There are also books (e.g., Questions #42, #43, #44, and #45 in this book) and independent online sources that describe these high-stakes tests in detail so you can get a good sense of what to expect.
  - ○ One thing you should expect on all achievement tests is to miss a lot of questions. Something like 80% of test takers miss more than 25% of the questions on any achievement test. So, you can know a lot and still not get a perfect score. Even really smart people miss many questions.
- **Practice.**

  Some tests have entire stand-alone exams you can take to get a feel for how you'll do and what the testing experience is like. For example, the SAT has the PSAT, a version of the test that you can take a year earlier (and is used by some scholarship programs). On their sites, these companies often provide practice exams and sample items, as well. There are also many books and whole training courses that provide practice opportunities. (See Question #47 for a discussion of whether to take a test prep course.)
- **Prepare on the day of the exam.**

  Get plenty of sleep. Eat a good breakfast. Dress comfortably. Do not pull an all-nighter in hopes of getting a last minute boost of knowledge. It is unlikely that cramming in the days leading up to test day will make a difference. After all, whatever study materials you are using are unlikely to include the exact questions or vocabulary terms or bits of info that are covered on the actual exam.

- **Engage in smart test-taking behaviors**.

  There are three sets of strategies to help boost your score:

  o *General test-taking strategies.* Pay attention to the time and pace yourself. If you are not sure of an answer, try to eliminate one or two answer options that you know are likely incorrect. If you are allowed to skip a question and then go back to it, don't forget to go back!

  o *Writing essays.* Some achievement tests include an essay section where you write an original essay in response to some prompt. Take a few minutes to sketch an outline before starting to write. While it helps to use good compositional form with an introduction, organized body, and summarizing conclusion, there is research to suggest that certain other variables tend to result in higher scores. Longer essays score well, and essays with complex sentence structure and long sentences also do well.

  o *Choose when to guess.* On the ACT, there is no penalty for guessing on a question and getting it wrong. So, there is no reason not to respond to every question, even if you are running out of time and have to blindly choose answers at random. On the SAT, you lose ¼ point for every wrong answer. From a gambling perspective, if you are choosing from four possible answers, there is no harm in guessing. If you can eliminate even one answer option before you guess, though, that decreases your risk considerably, and you should not hesitate to guess away.

More questions? See #39, #92, and #93.

How Do Test Preparation Courses Work?

Test preparation courses focus on getting you experience with the format of the test you will be taking, familiarizing you with the general knowledge domains and skills that the test will measure, and teaching you general and test-specific test-taking strategies designed to decrease your anxiety and make you more "test-wise." With that as a goal, these courses tend to be effective. For instance, research suggests that test preparation courses for the SAT can increase scores (on the 200–800 scale) by 10 to 20 points, with a few studies finding even larger gains of 80 to 100 points for the more intensive training courses. Of course, you may be able to do all the things these courses do yourself without help and without paying any money. Some, though, do find that the level of professional support encourages them to actually prepare in an organized way.

In reality, most people who take these courses have already taken the test. And they wish to take it again and get a higher score the next time. So, the real question from a measurement point of view is whether taking the course will, in fact, increase your score. The answer is, maybe. It all depends on the score you got the first time, the reliability of the test, and the quality of the test preparation course.

Of course, you can expect your score to vary naturally between test administrations even without taking any special training. Question #92 describes the standard error of measurement and provides the formula for calculating it. With less than perfect reliability and assuming that random error is normally distributed, measurement statisticians know that an observed test score is likely to vary a bit when a test is retaken. It might be a little higher than the last time or a little lower. Presumably, a test preparation course would nudge retest scores a bit higher and not lower, of course, but there tends to be a limited amount of improvement that is likely to occur. And there is less room for improvement the further above the mean a person's last score fell.

By knowing this average amount of random error, an interval or range within which a person's retest score is likely to fall 95% of the time can be computed. This range of likely score change is called the *95% confidence interval*:

95% Confidence Interval = ±1.96 (Standard Error of Measurement)

Without a huge amount of change in the underlying construct to be measured (which is unlikely from taking a test prep course alone), second attempts at a test will probably result in a score that is within the 95% confidence interval. High scores (e.g., 90th percentile and above) are even less likely to get much higher, and it doesn't matter if you've taken the best test preparation course in the world. This table shows the possible score range, the approximate standard error of measurement, and the 95% confidence interval for three achievement tests:

Test	Score Range	Standard Error of Measurement	95% Confidence Interval
ACT Composite	1–36	2 points	± 4 points
SAT	200–800	35 points	± 69 points
GRE Verbal or Quantitative	130–170	2 points	± 4 points
GRE Writing	0–6	0.4 points	± .78 points

More questions? See #92 and #93.

PART 6

INTELLIGENCE TESTS

What Are Some of the Commonly Used Intelligence Tests?

Though they are sometimes used by psychiatrists to evaluate adults, intelligence tests are most commonly given to children in the schools. Four of the most commonly administered intelligence tests are the *Wechsler Intelligence Scales for Children* (WISC), the *Woodcock-Johnson Test of Cognitive Abilities* (WJ), the *Kaufman Assessment Battery for Children* (*K-ABC*), and the *Stanford-Binet Intelligence Scales*. All of these tests are norm-referenced and given one-on-one.

The *Wechsler* intelligence test has been around in some form or another since 1939 and gone through several completely different versions. The most recent iteration for children age 7 through 16 is the *WISC-IV*. A total score based on many individual subtests produces a *Full Scale IQ*, which is meant to represent general intelligence. 100 is the average IQ score produced. The subtests cover verbal ability, reasoning, memory, and processing speed.

The *Woodcock-Johnson's* most recent edition is the *WJ-3*, and it can be used for almost anyone aged 2 through 90. A variety of subtests are available with a brief screening version requiring only three subscales, a commonly administered 10 subscale version, and a couple of extended formats with up to 31 different subscales. The three central dimensions assessed by the *WJ* are comprehension and knowledge about the world, fluid reasoning and problem-solving ability, and processing speed. Like the *Wechsler*, the average total score on the *Woodcock-Johnson* is 100.

The *Kaufman-ABC's* most recent form is the *KABC-II*. It is designed for children from age 3 to 18. Scores range from about 55 to about 145 on each subscale, with the average child scoring 100. Though it is a measure of cognitive development, it is not commonly used as a stand-alone intelligence test, but more often as a diagnostic tool for populations with unique characteristics, such as those with learning or cognitive disabilities. From 16 different subtests covering different ways of processing and reasoning, the test giver typically chooses four or five that will provide the most relevant information. Because it focuses more on problem-solving processes, and less on culture-bound content, the K-ABC tends not to find the same ethnic and racial differences that are often found with other cognitive ability tests.

The *Stanford-Binet Intelligence Scales* started it all. The first test to measure "intelligence" in a modern way by asking questions and assigning cognitive tasks, the *Stanford-Binet* began in France, and a U.S. version was developed in the 1910s. In its current form, the test produces a Full Scale IQ (the *Stanford-Binet* was the test that introduced the term and concept of IQ) along with a nonverbal and verbal IQ and several "factor" scores, such as visual-spatial processing and fluid reasoning. Like most standardized intelligence tests, scores are standardized to have a mean of 100 and, in its more recent versions, a standard deviation of 15.

More questions? See #49 and #50.

What Is an IQ?

A n *IQ* is a standardized score calculated using a formula based on the raw score one receives on an intelligence test. Though not every intelligence test calls its total score an IQ, many of the most popular tests do.

IQ stands for Intelligence Quotient, and there are two ways historically that the value has been computed. As part of a revised version of the first widespread intelligence test, the *Stanford-Binet Intelligence Test*, in 1916, the concept of an IQ score was introduced. The *Stanford-Binet* was (and is) made up of tasks and subtests that become less difficult as one grows older. To account for this, the total score that had been reported, an estimate of "Mental Age," was now modified by comparing it to one's actual chronological age. This first IQ formula was

$$IQ = 100 \times \textbf{Mental Age/Chronological Age}$$

For about 50 years, this formula was standard. One major flaw in this approach, though, was that typically developing children master the measured skills as teenagers (or, at least, reach a plateau in how well they can do), so their mental age stops at some level. People, of course, continue to get older, however. So, a 30-year-old person with the same cognitive abilities as a 40-year-old has a higher IQ! In the 1960s, this ratio approach to IQ scores was replaced by the major intelligence tests with a *Deviation IQ* score. Deviation IQs work the way most standardized scores work. They assume a normal curve. Deviation IQs convert individual raw scores onto a scale, which ensures that the mean will be 100 and the standard deviation will be (on most intelligence tests) 15. The modern formula for computing IQ scores makes use of Z-scores (see Question #87), which present raw scores as distances from the mean divided by the standard deviation of the distribution of raw scores. Today's IQ formula is

$$IQ = 100 + 15(Z)$$

IQ is not synonymous with *intelligence*. It is simply the common name for the scores produced by intelligence tests. Most IQ scores have these characteristics:

IQ Scores

Typical Range	Mean	Standard Deviation
55–145	100	15

More questions? See #50 and #58.

How Is Intelligence Usually Defined and Measured?

The word *intelligence* derives from a Latin term that essentially means the ability to discern or recognize. As used in common language and also as commonly defined by those who build and administer intelligence tests, though, intelligence usually means one of three characteristics (or a combination of these):

- Knowing stuff
- The ability to learn
- The ability to solve problems or puzzles

The makers of major intelligence tests apply an operational definition of intelligence that is consistent with these attributes when they create questions and tasks for the various subtests that make up their instruments.

The earliest widespread intelligence test, the *Stanford-Binet Intelligence Scales*, was made up of a group of activities that schoolteachers believed represented important skills for doing well in school and separated typically developing students from those with intellectual disabilities. The key abilities were *attention to detail, verbal ability*, and *memory*. Memory capacity and verbal skill have remained two major dimensions of intelligence as measured across most tests of cognitive ability.

The widely used *Wechsler* intelligence tests define intelligence as a single trait that underlies and explains performance across many school-related (and job-related) skills that are commonly treated as evidence of intelligence. This approach derives from the predominant theory of intelligence, first espoused by psychologist Charles Spearman in 1904, known as "General *g*" theory. It's the idea that while intelligence may be reflected by a variety of abilities, a single construct, *g*, accounts for performance. Most intelligence tests explicitly or implicitly derive from this belief, and the performance across the subtests on almost any intelligence tests will tend to correlate together, suggesting the existence of *g*.

Not all tests define intelligence as *general g*. Some exceptions are tests like the *Kaufman Assessment Battery for Children*, which views intelligence as the ability to solve problems in two distinctive ways—simultaneously or sequentially—or measures based on the psychologist Howard Gardner's theories that there are many different types of "intelligence" that are valuable in different contexts across different cultures.

More questions? See #48 and #58.

How Is the Validity of an Intelligence Test Established?

All four of the approaches to validity evidence discussed in this book— content validity (Question #9), criterion validity (Question #10), construct validity (Question #11), and consequential validity (Question #12)—are used to demonstrate the validity of intelligence tests.

For example, the developers of the *Stanford-Binet* intelligence tests argue for content validity by describing the item development process. Experts were consulted (including educators), several pilot studies and "tryouts" were conducted, and an extensive "beta testing" period was applied to make sure that all the questions and tasks were appropriate and would work in real-life testing contexts.

Demonstrating criterion validity by correlating the scores from an intelligence test with scores from other measures is a standard validity strategy. For example, the makers of the *Kaufman-ABC-II* present evidence of a pattern of expected small-to-moderate correlations with tests of academic achievement and other measures of school performance.

Construct validity is particularly important for intelligence tests because of the controversial nature of any definition of the trait. Many test developers examine the internal structure of their tests to demonstrate that items and subtests tend to group together in ways consistent with their test's theories. For instance, the *Wechsler* scales have published analyses demonstrating that subtests within the same category have higher correlations with each other than with subtests from a different domain.

Issues of consequential validity for intelligence tests tend to focus on whether there is cultural bias (see Questions #13 and #14). Developers of the *Stanford-Binet* are typical in the steps they take to demonstrate that different cultures or demographic groups are not affected negatively by taking their test. In the test development process, items are reviewed for fairness in regard to race, ethnicity, gender, and religious background. In addition, statistical analyses are conducted on items to identify any apparent bias, and those items are removed.

More questions? See #8 and #11.

How Is the Reliability of an Intelligence Test Established?

O f the types of reliability discussed in this book, the only type of evidence not relevant for intelligence test scores are estimates of *parallel forms reliability* (see Question #24). That's because there aren't parallel forms used for intelligence tests. Most tests have a single, closely guarded version of their test.

Internal reliability is important for any group of items that are summed together to produce a scale score (see Question #21). Because high-stakes decisions are made based on intelligence tests, it is particularly important to establish that scores are very precise. For that reason, test developers almost always create very long tests with many items (a typical intelligence test administration can take an hour and a half). Consequently, internal reliability estimates tend to be very high. Typical are the internal reliability estimates reported by the *Wechsler* intelligence test for adults. Internal consistency for the Full Scale IQ score is about .97, and the subtest internal reliabilities range from .71 to .96.

Because many items on intelligence tests have a range of points possible depending on the quality of the answer or task performance, inter-rater reliability (see Question #23) is an important aspect of reliability for intelligence tests. There are no multiple-choice questions on individually administered intelligence tests, so there is some subjectivity in scoring. Most intelligence tests provide evidence in their manuals that they have established inter-rater reliability. For example, the *Stanford-Binet* manual reports a study that demonstrated correlations among pairs of scorers with an average of .90, which indicates very high consistency.

A third critical reliability argument concerns test-retest reliability (see Question #22). Intelligence is believed to be a trait that should remain fairly stable over time. So, one would expect that IQ scores should remain fairly consistent and not fluctuate between test occasions. For instance, the *Kaufman-ABC* intelligence test reports that with 2 to 4 weeks between administrations, test-retest correlations averaged about .87 for the broad total scores and between .59 and .98 for subtests.

More questions? See #17 and #21.

What Is the *Wechsler* Intelligence Test?

There are actually three *Wechsler* intelligence tests, one for preschoolers, one for children, and one for adults. The current versions of these tests are

- *Wechsler Preschool and Primary Scale of Intelligence, Fourth Edition* (WPPSI-IV)
- *Wechsler Intelligence Scale for Children, Fourth Edition* (WISC-IV)
- *Wechsler Adult Intelligence Scale, Fourth Edition* (WAIS-IV)

Collectively, they are the most commonly administered intelligence tests, and it is likely that if you hear about someone taking an IQ test, it is a *Wechsler Intelligence Scale* that is being referred to.

All three forms of the Wechsler use the same definition of intelligence as *the aggregate or global capacity of the individual to act purposefully, to think rationally, and to deal effectively with his or her environment*. In practice, this means that intelligence is treated as a single construct with a broad total score as the best measure of cognitive ability, the *Full Scale IQ*. Even though the test is developed based on an assumption of intelligence as a single trait, different subtests can be combined in a variety of ways for diagnostic purposes to identify strengths and weaknesses. There are two subscores that are produced focusing on verbal ability and performance-based problem-solving skills, *verbal IQ* and *performance IQ*. Even below those scores, there are a further four subscores that combine several subtests together to produce ability estimates in the specific areas of *verbal comprehension, perceptual reasoning, working memory,* and *processing speed.* The subtests focus on those sorts of cognitive skills that are necessary to learn, do well in school, and live independently as an adult.

All the scores produced by the various *Wechsler Intelligence Scales* are standardized on a scale with an average of 100. Scores above 100 indicate higher intelligence than average, while scores below 100 indicate intelligence less than average. For practical assessment purposes, only scores above 130 or below 70 are usually treated as out of the ordinary. About 95% of people score in this range. Here are the characteristics of *Wechsler* intelligence test scores:

Full Scale IQ

Typical Range	Mean	Standard Deviation
55–145	100	15

Here is a sample item from an earlier version of the *WISC*:

In what ways are an apple and banana alike?

(Answer: The best answers include the fact that they are both fruits.)

More questions? See #48 and #49.

What Is the *Woodcock-Johnson* Intelligence Test?

T he *Woodcock-Johnson Test of Cognitive Abilities* is designed for almost every age from 2 to 90. A "standard battery" includes 10 subtests, with a variety of additional tests that can be included for more specific identification of abilities. Though a combination of scores on all subtests is believed to measure the "general *g*" single dimension of intelligence (see Question #50), the *Woodcock-Johnson* is designed based on a theory of intelligence that identifies three key aspects of intelligence (defined by several more specific "factors"):

- **Comprehension-Knowledge**

  This is a "crystallized" stable body of knowledge, the result of learning.

- **Fluid Reasoning**

  "Fluid" describes a general level of rational problem-solving ability.

- **Processing Speed**

  How quickly can one complete detailed, concentrated tasks?

The most recent form of the test, the *WJ-III*, includes these 10 basic subtests:

Subtest	Factor Assessed
1. Verbal Comprehension	Comprehension-Knowledge
2. Visual-Auditory Learning	Long-Term Retrieval
3. Spatial Relations	Visual-Spatial Thinking
4. Sound Blending	Auditory Processing
5. Concept Formation	Fluid Reasoning
6. Visual Matching	Processing Speed
7. Numbers Reversed	Short-Term Memory
8. Incomplete Words	Auditory Processing
9. Auditory Working Memory	Short-Term Memory
10. Visual-Auditory Learning (Delayed)	Long-Term Retrieval

Standardized scores from the *Woodcock-Johnson* follow the now common scaling used for most intelligence tests with 100 as the average score. Here are the characteristics of *Woodcock-Johnson* intelligence test scores:

WJ-III Standard Scores

Typical Range	Mean	Standard Deviation
55–145	100	15

Here is an example of the type of items found on the *WJ-III*:

What goes in the blank? (Read aloud to the test taker). "Meow!" said the _____ as it chased after the mouse.

(Answer: Cat.)

More questions? See #48 and #49.

What Is the *Kaufman-ABC* Intelligence Test?

The *Kaufman Assessment Battery for Children* (K-ABC) differs in a couple of ways from most intelligence tests. First, it is designed to be diagnostic. Beyond simply producing a measure of general intelligence, the *K-ABC* was developed as a tool for identifying strengths and deficits in mental processing skills. Second, the *K-ABC* was originally based on *right brain/left brain* research along with a theory that the brain functions in both a sequential way and a simultaneous (multitasking) way. This neurological foundation has been augmented for the latest addition with the ability to interpret results and choose subtests based on the "crystalized and fluid intelligence" theory, which drives the *Woodcock-Johnson* intelligence test (see Question #54).

The latest version of the test, the *K-ABC-II*, includes these subtests from which the test giver chooses based on the purpose of the assessment and the test taker's age:

Simultaneous	Sequential	Planning	Learning	Knowledge
Triangles (Patterns)	Word Order	Pattern	Atlantis Names	Riddles
Face Recognition	Number Recall	Reasoning	Atlantis Delayed	Expressive
Block Counting	Hand	Story	Rebus	Vocabulary
Conceptual Thinking	Movements	Completion	Association	Verbal Knowledge
Rover (Mazes)			Rebus Delayed	
Gestalt Closure				
Pattern Reasoning				
Story Completion				

Like most intelligence tests, the *Kaufman Assessment Battery for Children* follows the now standard "mean of 100" score distribution. The characteristics of *K-ABC* scores are as follows:

K-ABC Scaled Scores

Typical Range	Mean	Standard Deviation
55–145	100	15

Here is an example of the type of task found on the *K-ABC-II*:

The child is given a small toy dog and is asked to place the dog on a printed maze and move him through the maze to a bone. Scoring is based on speed, following the rules, and success.

More questions? See #48 and #49.

What Is the *Stanford-Binet* Intelligence Test?

The *Stanford-Binet Intelligence Scales* has been around for more than 100 years and has been the traditional "IQ test" that is referred to in movies, in *New Yorker* cartoons, and throughout popular culture. Though just one of many intelligence tests used today in the schools and in other psychological contexts, the *Stanford-Binet* started as the first, original structured intelligence test, which asked students questions and gave them a variety of cognitive tasks to perform and puzzles to solve.

Around 1900, Alfred Binet, a psychologist, and Theodore Simon, a medical student, were interested in studying mental retardation among French schoolchildren. Needing a measure of intelligence to help with identification, they spoke with schoolteachers and other experts to identify skills and tasks that could distinguish "normal" students from "abnormal students." The resulting collection of subtests included tests of verbal abilities, such as knowledge of vocabulary, memory tests, such as repeating long sentences, tests of quantitative understanding, such as placing different weights in order, and some psychomotor tasks such as cutting paper. The collection of tests was revised several times and brought to America along the way, while gaining the name *Stanford* (University)-*Binet*.

Today, the *Stanford-Binet Intelligence Scales, Fifth Edition* (SB5), consists of a collection of tasks and subscales that produce IQ scores on five dimensions:

- Fluid reasoning
- Knowledge
- Quantitative processing
- Visual-spatial processing
- Working memory

Scores on subtests are combined into a *verbal* and *nonverbal IQ*, and performance across all tasks can be summed to produce a *Full Scale IQ*. All scores are standardized to have the same mean and standard deviation. Here are the characteristics of *Stanford-Binet* IQ scores:

Full Scale IQ

Typical Range	Mean	Standard Deviation
55–145	100	15

Unlike most other intelligence tests, completely different questions or tasks are given for different ages. (This characteristic makes the test somewhat less commonly used in schools because comparisons across time are more difficult). Here are some sample questions from an older form of the *Stanford-Binet* meant for 4-year-olds:

1. *Fill in the missing word when asked, "Brother is a boy; sister is a ____"*

2. *"Why do we have houses?"*

More questions? See #48 and #49.

What Are Some Alternatives to the Traditional Intelligence Tests?

Intelligence tests are not without controversy (see Question #58). There is not wide acceptance for any particular definition of intelligence (which is why there are so many different intelligence tests), and, for some, there has long been concern that for their most common purpose (school identification of cognitive and learning disabilities), they don't even work particularly well. Consequently, there are a variety of alternative methods of measurement and identification of cognitive abilities. The alternatives can be categorized into three approaches:

- Applying a different, "better" definition of intelligence
- Measuring more specific relevant abilities instead of general intelligence
- Assessing cognitive and learning disabilities without relying on intelligence tests

The traditional definition of intelligence, shared to some extent by most of the major intelligence tests, is something along the lines of *a general ability to reason, solve problems, think abstractly, and learn from experience.* There are other definitions of intelligence that one could choose, however, such as psychologist Howard Gardner's view that intelligence is the ability to "solve problems or fashion products that are of consequence in a particular cultural setting or community" or psychologist Robert Sternberg's definition of "a mental activity directed toward purposive adaptation to, selection and shaping of, real-world environments relevant to one's life." These definitions allow for very individualized definitions of intelligence.

There are some cognitive tests that measure specific reasoning abilities relevant to specific diagnostic purposes or research questions but aren't concerned with a broad IQ score. For example, the *Mini-Mental State Examination* is a quick assessment of brain functioning to screen for disorientation, dementia, or brain injury. And the *Raven's Progressive Matrices* test presents a series of nonverbal visual tasks to measure abstract reasoning ability.

Intelligence tests are often used for special education identification. A newer approach for this sort of identification and for assessment during school-based interventions is *Curriculum-Based Assessment.* This approach uses direct observation of student performance within the classroom curriculum (e.g., assignments, tests, grades, and other assessment information) to generate instructional solutions. The strength of this approach is that it is a very direct way to test what is being taught. Frequently, pre- and postcomparisons are made to evaluate learning. More and more, federal policy that guides special education funding allows for curriculum-based assessment and other alternatives to intelligence testing to be used for classification and qualification.

More questions? See #51 and #58.

Why Are Intelligence Tests Controversial?

Even though the major intelligence tests are highly reliable and are generally considered valid under accepted standards, they have long been controversial. There are generally three issues of concern when the value of intelligence tests is questioned.

Intelligence tests are culture-dependent. It is difficult to define intelligence and choose items and tasks for an intelligence test without being influenced by the values and assumptions of the dominant culture in which the test is developed. Different races, ethnicities, and cultures perform differently on these tests, and consequently have different "IQs." This suggests that intelligence tests are not universally valid.

Is intelligence determined by genetics or environment? This is often framed as a debate of *nature versus nurture*. Researchers have long studied whether one's level of cognitive ability is determined based on nature (genetic predisposition at birth) or whether it is affected by nurture (the conditions in which one is raised). Does your DNA set the range for your ultimate intelligence, or is it the stimuli and learning opportunities in the world around you as you grow up? The current thinking is that it is likely a mix of the two influences. You inherit a general level of ability from mom and dad, but your eventual IQ can be affected by environmental factors such as interactions with parents and family, language-rich surroundings, and so on.

Intelligence as a measure of worth. Think of how we use words like *smart* and *stupid* in everyday conversation. It is common to treat the trait of intelligence as somehow a proxy for how valuable or useful a person is. A stinging insult among children is to accuse each other of having low intelligence. Intelligence, though, is just another characteristic of humans, like height or shyness. How well a person would score on an IQ test is not a measure of their goodness or worth as an individual. The early intelligence tests helped foster this name-calling, by the way, with official categories based on low IQ scores of *imbecile, idiot,* and *moron.*

Ultimately, it is the assumptions of what intelligence is and how IQ scores are used to make decisions that have led to controversy. The intended purpose of most intelligence tests is to predict how well a child will do in school, how well someone can take care of herself, or how one will perform in the world of work. And, for those purposes, intelligence tests actually do a pretty good job.

More questions? See #50 and #51.

PART 7

PERSONALITY TESTS AND ATTITUDE SCALES

What Do Personality Tests Measure?

*P*ersonality is the term used by psychologists for that fairly stable set of character traits defining our feelings, behaviors, and tendencies. Personality tests are usually made up of a set of questions for individuals to respond to (or tasks to perform), and those responses are combined in some meaningful way to assess those personality traits. We will use the term *personality test* very broadly to include all those psychological assessments used to measure a range of attributes from attitude to patterns of thinking to mental illness.

There are a couple of common formats for personality tests. The most popular and most straightforward approach is to ask test takers about their thoughts and their attitudes. These *self-report* strategies often ask people to indicate a range of agreement or disagreement with statements about themselves or other people. A second, less common, personality test format is based on a theory of *projection*, the idea that our unconscious thoughts and drives (of which we may not even be aware) can be made visible when we are asked to respond to some stimuli. References to personality tests in pop culture are usually to these sorts of projective tests, such as "inkblot tests" (where respondents are shown an apparently meaningless pattern and asked what they see) or free association tests ("I'll say a word, and you tell me the first thing that comes into your mind").

The table below shows some popular personality tests and what they are intended to measure:

Test	Format	What Is It Supposed to Measure?
MMPI (Minnesota Multiphasic Personality Inventory)	Self-report	Mental health
Rorschach Inkblot Test	Projective	Unconscious thinking revealed by interpreting abstract patterns
NEO Personality Inventory	Self-report	Five key personality traits, **n**euroticism, **e**xtraversion, **o**penness to experience, agreeableness, conscientiousness
Thematic Apperception Test	Projective	Unconscious attitudes revealed by describing scenes of people

Test	Format	What Is It Supposed to Measure?
Myers-Briggs Type Indicator	Self-report	Preferences for making decisions and perceiving the world
Draw-a-Person Test	Projective	In children and adolescents, their cognitive development in terms of self and identity

More questions? See #2 and #8.

QUESTION #60

How Is the Validity of a Personality Test Established?

Because personality tests are designed to measure complex psychological traits that are difficult to observe directly, most strategies for establishing validity center on construct validity (see Question #11). Traditional research-based construct validity arguments that compare groups, especially diagnostic groups, are common, but sometimes *criterion* validity evidence is used as part of a broader *construct* validity case. Three of the personality measures examined in this book can act as illustrations of the approaches that developers of personality tests (and those who use them in research) take to establish validity.

The *Diagnostic and Statistical Manual of Mental Disorders* (*DSM*) provides descriptions and checklists of criteria to identify mental disorders (see Question #65 for a discussion on the complexities involved in validating a diagnosis of mental illness). While not a test, strictly speaking, it is an assessment system that still must establish validity to demonstrate its usefulness. Construct validity arguments for the *DSM* are often theory based. That is, it is argued that the criteria that define any particular disorder are derived from research, collective experience of professionals, and theory. The fact that the definitions of disorders, and the classifications of whether a given pattern of thinking and behaving even *is* a disorder, change from version to version of the *DSM* is a validity concern that is frequently cited.

The *Minnesota Multiphasic Personality Inventory* (MMPI) is used to identify personality disorders and mental illness. Different traits are assessed by different subscales. Construct validity is, potentially, a bit problematic for the MMPI because many of the scales were developed atheoretically. That is, different patterns of responses that identified different personality types were placed together on scales whether there was any theoretical explanation for the pattern or not. Construct validity arguments for the MMPI tend to emphasize how well the test discriminates between different groups of people with diagnosed personality disorders.

The *Beck Depression Inventory* (BDI) (see Question #67) is a commonly used Likert-type scale to screen for depression. It is not meant to replace a more structured diagnostic approach, such as the *DSM*, but does need to establish that it is measuring the underlying construct of depression. The developers and researchers have provided construct validity evidence by demonstrating that there is an association between how people score on the *Beck* and how they score on other measures of depression. There are also major differences in mean scores between those who have been diagnosed with depression and the general population. Another construct validity argument for the *BDI* is that scores do not highly correlate with measures of similar constructs that are theoretically different. For example, the *Beck* only correlates moderately with measures of anxiety.

More questions? See #2 and #8.

How Is the Reliability of a Personality Test Established?

As with any test made up of multiple items combined to produce single scale scores, internal reliability is one aspect of reliability that is necessary to establish for personality tests (see Question #21). For personality scores, though, a second type of reliability, test-retest reliability, is critical, as well (see Question #22). Personality tests often measure traits, and *traits*, by definition, are not supposed to change very much or very easily across time. So, it is important to demonstrate high test-retest reliability for whatever is being measured. Two of the tests described in this book, the *Minnesota Multiphasic Personality Inventory* (MMPI) and the *Beck Depression Inventory* (BDI), can act as illustrations for what is typically reported as reliability evidence for personality tests.

Internal reliability estimates for these sorts of scales are usually reported as coefficient alphas, a value that ranges from 0 to 1.0, with values above .70 considered good for research purposes. Higher reliability estimates would frequently be expected for personality tests when high-stakes decisions are being made, however. In terms of internal consistency, the various scales on the MMPI are typically found to demonstrate reliability in the high .7's to low .8's range. The BDI, which is a single 21-item scale, demonstrates high reliability with estimates around .92.

For test-retest reliability, researchers correlate performance on a scale with scores received on a second administration some time later. For the MMPI, test-retest coefficients are relatively good when a few weeks have passed. Correlations around .75 have been reported. College-aged and younger adults tend to show somewhat less stability in scores than those in older populations, which is consistent with how personality traits usually work. Researchers using the Beck have reported 1-week test-retest reliability estimates of .93. This is very high and a bit surprising because it was with a college population whose depression scores tend to fluctuate.

More questions? See #17 and #18.

What Are the Different Ways to Measure Attitude?

You might think the best way to find out how someone feels is to ask them "How do you feel about this?" but their responses will be so varied and hard to quantify that it would be difficult to analyze responses statistically in the ways that social science research prefers. Instead, those who wish to measure attitude have developed a variety of formats that, strangely enough, usually do not ask questions at all.

Let's start with a definition of attitude, which distinguishes it from something more stable and central to identity like a personality trait. An attitude is an emotional position toward a fact, object, or idea. Attitudes have some effect on behavior (though not a strong effect, as personality researchers often discover to their consternation) but can change fairly easily.

Questions 94 to 100 provide many more specific examples of *how* to measure attitude, but the general strategy can be summarized here. The standard way for measuring attitude is to present an attitude statement, such as "I like the taste of eggs!" and ask respondents to indicate whether they agree or disagree with the statement. People, of course, don't always report their attitude accurately, but the apparent directness of this measurement strategy is hard to beat. The format by which people indicate their agreement differs between the two common approaches to attitude measurement.

The most common format for measuring attitude is known as a **Likert**-type item. Likert was the social scientist who developed the approach in the 1930s (and he pronounced his name "LICK-ert"). You've seen Likert items. They look like this:

Indicate the extent to which you agree or disagree with the statement below. I like the taste of eggs.

Strongly Disagree	Disagree	Neither Agree nor Disagree	Agree	Strongly Agree
1	2	3	4	5

What makes this a Likert item is that the answer options are balanced with roughly equal appearing psychological or quantitative distances between each answer option. Question #63 explores this format further.

Another attitude survey format that has better measurement properties, but is much less popular than Likert-type items, is the **Thurstone** approach. Named for another social scientist who suggested the method in the late 1920s, Thurstone scales present a variety of attitude statements and simply ask respondents to indicate which statements they agree with, but not how much they agree. Instead of the answer options ranging in strength and point value as with Likert-type items, it is the statements themselves that range in strength and point value (typically from 1 to 11 points), and they can be positive or negative. So a four-item Thurstone scale might look like this (without the point values being shown):

Place a checkmark next to each statement with which you agree.

_____ *Eggs taste unpleasant.*   [2 Points]

_____ *I don't mind eggs occasionally, but they aren't my favorite.* [6 Points]

_____ *I like the taste of eggs.*   [9 Points]

_____ *Eggs are the best food ever!*   [11 Points]

The point value of each statement is determined by a group of judges. Question #64 describes this process in detail.

There is more work required in developing a Thurstone attitude scale than there is for writing Likert-type items. This is likely why it is the Likert format that is so widely used.

More questions? See #59 and #94.

How Do I Construct My Own Likert-Type Attitude Scale?

As Question #62 describes, Likert-type attitude items present statements and allow people to indicate how much they agree or disagree with each statement along a continuum of answer options. A group of these items can be written and their responses summed (or, better yet, averaged) to produce a reliable score representing a single dimension or construct: *attitude toward (something)*.

Some basic guidelines for formatting Likert items are the following:

- There are typically four to seven options. Five answer options, with a neutral middle, is very common, but a middle answer option is not required.
- If a middle answer option is used, it is best to word it in a way that suggests that the respondent has an attitude that is in the "middle" of the range from disagree to agree. For example, "Neutral" is a common label, as is "Neither Agree nor Disagree." A middle or neutral attitude is not necessarily the same as having *no* attitude about something.
- To "force" respondents to place themselves on one side or the other of an issue, researchers will sometimes choose to have an even number of answer options. This eliminates the possibility of choosing the middle ground. This also may increase variability (which can benefit reliability; see Question #17).
- All options usually have labels, although sometimes only a few are offered and the others are implied. For instance, researchers might only label the *anchors*, the two answer options at either end of the continuum.
- In scoring, numbers are assigned to each option (such as 1 to 5). There is no hard-and-fast rule, but, most commonly, higher scores indicate a more positive attitude.

The Likert scoring system is meant to be at a high level of measurement. In Question #3, we pointed out how if one can measure at the interval level (equal meaning and quantity between each adjacent pair of scores), a lot of information can be represented with those scores, and powerful statistical analyses can be conducted. Most that use the Likert approach treat the level of measurement as interval, though some argue that while it is clearly *ordinal* (there is a difference in quantity across answer options), there may not be equal "distance" between each pair of answer options. For instance, is there the same amount of "attitude" difference between strongly agree and agree as there is between strongly disagree and disagree? Most statisticians, though, are more concerned about whether scores are normally distributed than whether they are technically at the interval level or ordinal level. And Likert-type scores, especially when they are combined across many items into a total scale score, tend to be normally distributed.

Here are examples of the three most common formats for Likert-type attitude items:

5-Point Traditional Likert Item

	Strongly Disagree	Disagree	Neither Agree nor Disagree	Agree	Strongly Agree
I like eggs.	1	2	3	4	5

Likert Item With Only Anchors Labeled

	Disagree				Agree
I like eggs.	1	2	3	4	5

Likert Item With No Middle Option

	Strongly Disagree	Disagree	Agree	Strongly Agree
I like eggs.	1	2	3	4

More questions? See #60, #62, and #95.

How Do I Construct My Own Thurstone Attitude Scale?

Question #62 introduced Thurstone-type attitude scales. A Thurstone scale has a number of statements to which the respondent is asked to agree or disagree. The statements have been previously weighted so that stronger statements are worth more points than weaker statements.

These different score values of statements are determined by "judges" who are asked to sort a large number of statements into groups ranging from "shows weak support for the attitude" to "shows strong support for the attitude." The median score across judges becomes the point value for each statement. Scores usually range from 1 to 11.

Thurstone scaling appears to create interval-level scaling. Among hardcore statisticians, this is important because they can conduct statistical analyses using scores derived from Thurstone scales without worry about whether the level of measurement isn't really only ordinal, a concern for some who use Likert-type formats (see Question #63).

Here's how to develop your own Thurstone scale.

1. Choose an attitudinal object, something you can write opinion statements about.

   Example

   Eggs

2. Write dozens of attitudinal statements. As you compose these statements, try to create a range of attitude levels. Write some statements that are very positive, some that are moderately positive, some that are moderately negative, and some that are strongly negative. For example,

Strongly positive	*I love eggs more than anything!*
Moderately positive	*I like eggs.*
Moderately negative	*I'm not a big egg fan.*
Strongly negative	*I really hate eggs!*

3. Get a panel of "judges" (any smart people). Give them each statement and ask them to rate each statement on a 1 to 11 scale in terms of how *strongly worded* the statement is. Traditionally, they "rate" them by creating 11 different piles and placing the items into the piles representing those different strengths. The piles should be based on this scale:

1	2	3	4	5	6	7	8	9	10	11

Strongly   Neutral   Strongly
Negatively   Positively
Worded   Worded

Remember: It doesn't matter whether they personally agree or disagree with the statement; the judges are asked only to rate the statement in terms of the *words* used. How strong a statement is it?

4. Collect the piles and average the ratings (determined by the pile in which the statement was placed) across judges for each statement. These averages become the weights for the statements; they are the point value or score for each statement.

5. Choose at least 11 statements that cover a wide range of point values (or weights). These statements are your Thurstone scale.

6. Unlike on Likert scales, respondents are only asked to indicate which statements they agree with. They are not rating their agreement with the statements. You score your scale by adding together the point values (or weights) *only* for those statements with which they agree. Higher values indicate a more positive attitude toward the attitude object. Lower values indicate a more negative attitude.

More questions? See #63 and #95.

How Are Mental Disorders Diagnosed?

While many of the tests discussed in this book produce scores that are directly tied to a well-defined fairly simple construct, few such measures exist for identifying, diagnosing, or "scoring" mental illnesses or disorders. The common approach for official diagnosis involves a great deal of subjectivity both in application and in defining the personality constructs themselves. To make this inherently fuzzy process as concrete and objective as possible, mental health professionals rely on the *Diagnostic and Statistical Manual of Mental Disorders* (*DSM*).

The *DSM* (Version 5 was released in 2013) provides a checklist of criteria that in mostly observable, behavioral ways "define" a variety of mental disorders. The criteria have been chosen based on theory and changing understanding of these disorders by members of the *American Psychiatric Association*. The manual is primarily used to place patients and clients into categories for the purposes of identifying useful treatments, but it is also generally required for determination of health insurance coverage.

Traditionally, psychiatric diagnoses under the *DSM* system have been grouped into five categories, dimensions, or "axes." They are

- Axis I: All diagnostic categories except mental retardation and personality disorder
- Axis II: Personality disorders and mental retardation
- Axis III: General medical condition; acute medical conditions and physical disorders
- Axis IV: Psychosocial and environmental factors contributing to the disorder
- Axis V: Global assessment for children and teens under the age of 18

Here is an example of *DSM* criteria, in this case, for depression:

- Depressed mood or a loss of interest or pleasure in daily activities for more than 2 weeks
- Mood represents a change from the person's baseline.

- Impaired function: social, occupational, educational
- Specific symptoms, at least five of these nine, present nearly every day:

1. Depressed mood or irritable most of the day, nearly every day, as indicated by either subjective report (e.g., feels sad or empty) or observation made by others (e.g., appears tearful)

2. Decreased interest or pleasure in most activities, most of each day

3. Significant weight change (5%) or change in appetite

4. Change in sleep: insomnia or hypersomnia

5. Change in activity: psychomotor agitation or retardation

6. Fatigue or loss of energy

7. Guilt/worthlessness: feelings of worthlessness or excessive or inappropriate guilt

8. Concentration: diminished ability to think or concentrate, or more indecisiveness

9. Suicidality: thoughts of death or suicide, or has suicide plan

More questions? See #59 and #60.

What Is the MMPI Personality Test?

The *Minnesota Multiphasic Personality Inventory* (MMPI) is a test used by professionals to identify personality disorders and mental illness. It consists of 10 subscales, and each assesses a category of human traits and behavior.

The items are statements to which a person responds as to whether each is true about him or her. There are many hundreds of items, some of which seem to directly assess pathology and some that seem unrelated to any personality variables. Different patterns of responses, even unobvious patterns, have been found to be related to different clinically diagnosed conditions. These are not actual items from the *MMPI*, but they are similar:

I am often nervous.

I like magazines about motorcycles.

I wish there weren't so many laws.

The current form of the MMPI includes these scales each designed to assess particular aspects of personality or type of personality disorder:

Scale	Focus
Hypochondriasis	Concern with bodily symptoms
Depression	Depressive symptoms
Hysteria	Awareness of problems and vulnerabilities
Psychopathic Deviate	Conflict, struggle, anger, respect for society's rules
Masculinity/Femininity	Stereotypical masculine or feminine interests/behaviors
Paranoia	Level of trust, suspiciousness, sensitivity
Psychasthenia	Worry, anxiety, tension, doubts, obsessiveness
Schizophrenia	Odd thinking and social alienation
Hypomania	Level of excitability
Social Introversion	People orientation

Scores from the MMPI are standardized into *T*-scores (see Question #88) with a mean of 50 and a standard deviation of 10. Scores on any scale tend to range between 20 and 80. Scores that are unusually high or low are considered clinically significant.

A unique aspect of the MMPI is that in addition to the 10 major scales, there are also several "validity" scales that assess how honest the test taker has been and other aspects of his or her attitude toward taking the exam. The questions are designed to detect whether respondents are exaggerating or (downplaying) the severity of psychological symptoms and whether their responses are consistent.

More questions? See #62 and #88.

How Is Depression Measured?

F or a formal diagnosis of depression, mental health professionals most often rely on the *Diagnostic and Statistical Manual of Mental Disorders* (*DSM*). For purposes of informal assessment, for research, or as a screening instrument, though, there are several brief checklists and attitude scales useful for measuring the construct of depression. Several screening instruments are used to assess levels of depression at the population level. For instance, both the *Center for Epidemiologic Studies Depression Scale* (CESD) and the World Health Organization's *Composite International Diagnostic Interview* (CIDI) are based on the *DSM*'s criteria. One of the most widely used scales for individual screening is the *Beck Depression Inventory* (BDI), developed by the cognitive-behavioral psychologist Aaron Beck, and we will focus on that measure here.

The most recent version of the *Beck Depression Inventory* consists of 21 Likert-type (see Question #63) items that focus on the test takers' feelings toward the future, toward themselves, and toward the whole world. Answer options for each item are scaled from 0 to 3 points, with higher scores indicating greater depression, so scores can range from 0 to 63.

Items from the *BDI-II* (the latest edition) cover areas such as sadness, interest in sex, tiredness, pessimism, and suicidal thoughts. Answer options are worded in similar ways; here is the sadness item from an earlier form of the test:

(0) I do not feel sad.

(1) I feel sad.

(2) I am sad all the time and I can't snap out of it.

(3) I am so sad or unhappy that I can't stand it.

Score interpretation follows these guidelines:

14–19	Mild depression
20–28	Moderate depression
29–63	Severe depression

This suggests that choosing the 1-point or greater answer on more than two thirds of the 21 items is reason for some mild concern with an average of 1 or above across all the items suggesting serious concern.

More questions? See #59 and #65.

How Are Alcoholism and Other Addictions Diagnosed?

Though alcohol and other drugs vary in their addiction characteristics, there are similar approaches commonly taken to determine if one is abusing a substance. Technically, a diagnosis of addiction likely comes from applying criteria set out in the *Diagnostic and Statistical Manual of Mental Disorders* (*DSM*), published by the *American Psychiatric Association*. To determine if one has a "problem" with a substance, whether officially diagnosed or not, there are several checklists and attitude scales that can be used.

The *DSM* defines alcoholism (actually "alcohol dependence") as

A pattern of alcohol use leading to serious problems, as indicated by three or more of the following at any time during one 12-month period:

- Increased tolerance for alcohol, it takes more and more to make you feel drunk
- Feeling sick or anxious when you cut down or stop drinking
- Drinking more alcohol or for a longer period of time than you planned
- Wishing you could cut back or stop your drinking, but not being able to
- Spending much of your time drinking, getting alcohol, or recovering after drinking
- Quitting or missing important social or job activities because of your drinking
- Continuing to use alcohol, even though it's causing problems in your life

There are dozens of survey instruments and other protocols that assess whether drinking is a problem. A typical approach is the one used by the *Alcohol Use Disorders Identification Test* (*AUDIT*). The AUDIT was developed by the World Health Organization as a short screening instrument to help identify whether alcohol use is harmful for a person. There are 10 items that ask about alcohol use. Questions on the AUDIT include the following:

How often do you have a drink containing alcohol?

(0) *Never*

(1) *Monthly or less*

(2) *2 to 4 times a month*

(3) *2 to 3 times a week*

(4) *4 or more times a week*

How often during the last year have you had a feeling of guilt or remorse after drinking?

(0) *Never*

(1) *Less than monthly*

(2) *Monthly*

(3) *Weekly*

(4) *Daily or almost daily*

How often during the last year have you failed to do what was normally expected from you because of drinking?

(0) *Never*

(1) *Less than monthly*

(2) *Monthly*

(3) *Weekly*

(4) *Daily or almost daily*

The number of points each answer is worth are those shown next to the answer. So, for 10 items, the maximum score is 40. Total scores above 20 suggest the possibility of a drinking problem, and further assessment is suggested.

More questions? See #59 and #60.

PART 8

CLASSROOM ASSESSMENT

How Do I Decide What to Assess in My Classroom?

S choolteachers have a lot of assessment decisions to make in today's class-rooms. Chief among them is figuring out what to assess. What do they want their students to learn? Two approaches that can help with these decisions are *Bloom's taxonomy* and *backward design.*

A classic theoretical framework suggested by educational researcher Benjamin Bloom categorizes levels of learning into six different cognitive stages. His classification system thinks of learning as developmental, with students moving through six potential stages of understanding. The six levels are the following:

1. **Knowledge.** This is simple recall of memorized information.

2. **Comprehension.** Truly *understanding* what is being communicated.

3. **Application.** Ability to apply knowledge and understanding to solve problems and answer questions not seen before.

4. **Analysis.** Identifying the parts of an idea or process and understanding the relationships among the parts.

5. **Synthesis.** The creative act of putting pieces together to make a new product, pattern, or idea.

6. **Evaluation.** Ability to make meaningful judgments about the value of ideas, products, or processes.

Assessments can be planned to get at whichever level of understanding is consistent with a teacher's goals.

Another helpful strategy for classroom teachers to identify the most important learning objectives for their students is to apply what teaching expert Grant Wiggins calls *backward design.* Instead of starting with the instructional activity that a teacher wishes to use, linking that to an objective, and, finally, creating some sort of assessment to measure whether learning occurred (a real-life sequence of lesson planning that Wiggins believes is common), backward-design principles suggest a different order of things. Start by identifying the few most important learning outcomes for your students. These are those concepts or skills that have enduring value—they provide a foundation for future learning or are basic ideas that ensure deep understanding of a subject. Next, figure out how to make learning visible.

This is the assessment step. If your students did master a skill or truly understood a concept, how would you know? Finally, as the *last* step, not the first step, choose an instructional activity that will increase the skill or understanding.

More questions? See #8 and #9.

What Are the Different Types of Assessment I Can Use?

If a classroom teacher wishes to assess his or her students' learning, there are several different approaches to choose from. The right way to go depends on the purpose of the assessment and the philosophy of the teacher.

The most common type of assessment that students face remains *traditional paper-and-pencil assessment*. This is the somewhat vague term used to describe those formats that have objective scoring and are made up of questions with right or wrong answers. Formats such as multiple-choice and matching are traditional paper-and-pencil formats. They work best for measuring basic knowledge.

Another popular format for classroom assessment specializes in measuring students' skills, abilities, and deep understanding. Performance-based assessment requires students to produce something (such as a composition or a painting) or perform in some way (such as giving a speech or conducting a scientific experiment). The scoring of these assessments tends to be subjective and multifaceted.

If the purpose of the assessment isn't to measure how much learning has occurred, but instead to give feedback about whether students and teachers are on the right track while instruction is still going on, then *formative assessment* is the approach for you. Formative assessment allows students to see where they're at in terms of understanding concepts or developing skills. It also allows teachers to evaluate the effectiveness of their teaching and change direction or strategies before a topic or unit is done. Notice that formative assessment doesn't affect your grade, which is a very modern twist on the purpose of testing.

Recently, many educators have become concerned about the artificial nature of classroom assessment, especially the traditional paper-and-pencil approaches. After all, it's only in classrooms that people are usually asked to respond to multiple-choice questions. It's not a skill you tend to use much in the real world. Those who believe that assessment tasks should be consistent with real world expectations and measure those abilities that are valued in the real world argue that *authentic assessment* is the most valid testing philosophy.

A final approach to classroom assessment is consistent with the broader movement for accessibility in education. Just as schools are designed now so that all people can use them regardless of physical or educational disability, and teachers apply universal design principles when they teach so all can benefit, there is also a movement toward universal design in assessment. The goal is to design assessments that are equally valid for all students.

These different choices for types of classroom assessment aren't mutually exclusive, of course, and teachers can combine several of these approaches. Which type they choose depends on what is being assessed, how the information will be used, and what their philosophies are about tests and measurement.

More questions? See #8 and #9.

How Are the Validity and Reliability of Classroom Assessments Established?

There are a variety of types of validity evidence and a variety of types of reliability evidence (see Questions #8 and #17). For classroom assessment, the tests that teachers make themselves, there tends to be one aspect of validity that is most important, *content validity,* and one aspect of reliability that is most important, *inter-rater reliability.*

Content validity is the extent to which the questions or tasks on an assessment are a fair representation of the items that could or should be on the test. For teachers, there is usually a set of instructional objectives or state standards or some fairly formal list of what should be taught and what should be assessed. This acts as a convenient catalog of content that could be covered on a test and allows for a rather straightforward analysis of whether a classroom assessment is content valid.

For any particular test meant to cover a unit of instruction, many teachers build a *table of specifications.* Tables of specification lay out the different topics, content areas, or concepts that an assessment is meant to cover and indicate the number of questions or percentage of points or weights that each topic should be given. As an illustration, a simple table of specifications for a 10-question quiz over World War II might look like this:

	Topics		
	Allied Nations	Axis Nations	Causes and Consequences
Number of Questions	3	3	4

Inter-rater reliability, as described in Question #23, is concerned with the subjective nature of scoring. For classroom teachers, subjectivity is not a problem for most traditional paper-and-pencil tests (e.g., multiple-choice, matching formats) but is a concern when judgment is necessary.

Inter-rater reliability is often a worry for performance-based assessment, for example. The best way to decrease subjectivity when scoring classroom assessments and increase inter-rater reliability is to use a scoring rubric (see Question #78). Rubrics identify the key criteria for quality work in concrete, directly observable ways and provide a range of points possible for each criterion. They help guide teachers to more objective and consistent scoring.

If a teacher wished to establish some quantitative evidence of inter-rater reliability, he or she could do so. The simplest study would be to take two teachers and a few (e.g., 10) examples of student work, let's say essays, and have both teachers independently score the same pile of essays using the same scoring rubric. What percentage of the time did they agree on the right score to assign? That percentage acts as an estimate of inter-rater reliability for the scoring rubric. Agreement over 80% of the time is typically considered evidence of good reliability.

More questions? See #8 and #18.

What Are the Types of Traditional Paper-and-Pencil Test Items?

Traditional paper-and-pencil tests are made up of questions with right or wrong answers. The scoring is usually objective, which means that no judgment is necessary on the part of the scorer. Consequently, teachers like to use this format because scoring is quick; it's just a matter of comparing students' answers to an answer key. Large-scale test developers also like the format because these sorts of tests can be scored by computer. Four common types of traditional paper-and-pencil formats are *multiple-choice, matching items, fill-in-the-blank,* and *true-false* questions.

A multiple-choice question has a stem (the question that is asked) and several answer options, one of which (usually just one) is the right answer. Wrong answers are called distractors.

Here is an example of a multiple-choice question, with the different parts labelled:

Stem	1. In the *Harry Potter* series of books, by J. K. Rowling, what is the name of the dark wizard, often referred to as "he who must not be named"?
Distractor	A. Hagrid
Distractor	B. Weasley
Distractor	C. Dumbledore
Keyed or Correct Answer	D. Voldemort

Matching items have several stems or questions and several answer options from which to choose. The same answer options are available for each question. Students are asked to match the stem to the correct answer. Here is an example of a set of matching items:

_____ 1. Hagrid	A. Dark wizard "who must not be named"
_____ 2. Weasley	B. Harry's friend and classmate
_____ 3. Dumbledore	C. Half-giant groundskeeper of Hogwarts
_____ 4. Voldemort	D. Headmaster of Hogwarts

Note: Correct answers are 1-C, 2-B, 3-D, and 4-A.

Fill-in-the-blank items are sentences with key words missing. Students are asked to supply the missing words or missing information. Theoretically, guessing is much harder for fill-in-the-blank items because the possible answers aren't provided. Students must recall the answer, not just recognize it when they see it. Here is an example of a fill-in-the-blank question:

1. *In the* Harry Potter *series of books, by J. K. Rowling, the Dark wizard referred to as "he who must not be named" is Lord* _____.

True-false items present a statement and ask students to indicate whether the statement is true or false. They look like this:

For each statement about the Harry Potter *books, indicate whether it is True (T) or False (F).*

_____ 1. *Hagrid is the dark wizard who "must not be named."*

_____ 2. *Weasley is Harry's friend and classmate.*

_____ 3. *Dumbledore is the half-giant groundskeeper of Hogwarts.*

_____ 4. *Voldemort is the headmaster of Hogwarts.*

Note: Correct answers are 1-F, 2-T, 3-F, and 4-F.

Teachers choose from among these types and a few others, such as short answer, when they want easy-to-score questions that can cover a lot of basic knowledge pretty efficiently.

More questions? See #11, #69, and #70.

What Are the Characteristics of a Good Multiple-Choice Question?

Multiple-choice questions are traditionally the heart and soul of classroom tests. They are made up of a *stem*, the part that asks the question or provides the stimulus that requires a response, and *answer options*, just one of which (usually) is correct. The nature of these stems and answer options determines whether a multiple-choice question works the way it is supposed to work, whether it is valid. Researchers and measurement experts have offered dozens of suggestions and guidelines for writing a good multiple-choice item. The advice sometimes is contradictory because there is actually very little experimental research on whether various format and design choices make a difference, but there are some rules on which most agree. Here is a top 10 list of "rules" for writing multiple-choice questions:

1. **"All of the above" and "None of the above" should not be answer options.**

   There is a skill involved in being able to analyze all the answer options and figure out whether an "All of the above" or "None of the above" or "A and B, but not C" answer option is logically true. It is not likely, however, that this skill is an instructional objective that the test is designed to assess.

2. **All answer options should be plausible.**

   If an answer option isn't appealing to any student, it is not working as a useful distractor, and guessing the right answer suddenly becomes easier.

3. **Order of answer options should be unpredictable.**

   This prevents the "when in doubt, guess C" strategy from working.

4. **Items should cover important concepts and objectives.**

   This is obvious, right? Sometimes teachers, though, are tempted to write a question over something unimportant because it is a quick and easy question to write.

5. **Negative wording should not be used.**

   Students might get confused or overlook negative words like *not*.

6. **Answer options should all be grammatically consistent with the stem.**

   Don't give a grammatical clue that the right answer must start with a vowel, or be plural, or be a female, and so forth.

7. **Answer options should be homogeneous.**

   If all the answer options come from the same context or content area, they will all be equally plausible if a student has to guess at an answer.

8. **Stems must be unambiguous and clearly state the problem.**

   Sometimes students know the right answer, if only they could understand the question.

9. **Answer options should not be longer than the stem.**

   Put all the important complex information up front, so students can quickly process different answer options.

10. **The correct answer option should not be the longest answer option.**

    A test-wise student might know this old trick that the correct answer option tends to have the most words in it.

More questions? See #70, #71, and #72.

What Are the Characteristics
of a Good Matching Question?

Matching items consist of two parts, a long column of stems that act as the "questions" or terms looking for a match, and a long column of matches, or response options, or "answers" from which to choose. When creating your own set of matching questions, all the rules about multiple-choice questions apply (see Question #73), but there are some general guidelines specific to matching items that most measurement folks agree on:

1. **All the matching items should appear on the same page.**

   This keeps students from having to flip pages back and forth and possibly miss some options.

2. **Stems should be on the left and answer options on the right.**

   The "stem" for matching items refers to the part of the match that has the longest wording.

3. **There should be more answer options than stems, and answer options should be available more than once.**

   This lessens the chance of guessing.

4. **The number of answer options should be developmentally appropriate.**

   There should be fewer than about seven answer options in one matching section for elementary students and fewer than about 17 for secondary students.

5. **Matching item directions should include basis for match.**

   Instructions should provide some structure, such as "Match the battle to the year it occurred" or "Match the novel to the author."

6. **Answer options should be logically independent of one another.**

   Consideration of one answer option shouldn't rule out the possibility that all the unused options are still plausible.

Question #72 gives an example of a short quiz that uses the matching items format. It actually violates some of the rules provided here. Check it out and you'll see that the quiz ignores Suggestions 2 and 3 and, possibly, 5.

More questions? See #71 and #73.

What Are the Characteristics of a Good Fill-In-the-Blank Question?

Fill-in-the-blank items present a sentence that is incomplete because of one or more blanks that replace missing words or phrases. Students are asked to indicate, sometimes by actually writing them in, what words go in the blanks. Question #72 gives some examples of fill-in-the-blank items.

Of the traditional paper-and-pencil formats, fill-in-the-blank questions are among the more difficult to get the right answer by guessing. That's because they are not *selection* items, where the right answer is there and students must select it, such as with multiple-choice and matching items. They are *supply* items. Students must supply the right answer without any options there to jog their memory. As such, fill-in-the-blank items measure recall of information, not just recognition of information.

There are really only two agreed-upon rules specific to writing good fill-in-the-blank items, but they are biggies:

1. Use only one blank.

2. Put it at the end.

The idea behind both these recommendations is the same. For students to have a fair shot at showing what they know, there must be enough structure in the question itself to guide students toward an answer that they will know is right when they produce it. They can't be expected to magically read their teachers' minds and figure out what they're thinking.

For example, consider this fact that a teacher wishes his or her students to know:

The most common gas in the Earth's atmosphere is nitrogen.

One could write fill-in-the-blank questions to assess students' knowledge of this fact in many different ways. If a teacher has several instructional objectives related to this fact, including demonstrating knowledge of the definition of "atmosphere" and knowing that nitrogen is a gas and also knowing that it is the most common gas, he might be tempted to write a single item like this:

The most common _____ in the Earth's _____ is _____.

There are so many blanks or holes in this item that testing experts call this a *Swiss cheese item*. There is very little structure for a poor student to know what the teacher is after. For instance, this answer makes sense:

The most common <u>metal</u> in the Earth's <u>crust</u> is <u>silicon</u>.

Our teacher would count that wrong even though it demonstrates scientific knowledge and is a true statement (well, relatively true; silicon is actually a semimetal).

Slightly better would be something in this form:

The most common gas in the air around our planet is _____, which makes up 78% of our atmosphere.

Even that takes a bit of work to process because by putting the blank in the middle, students have to try each possible answer to see if it fits well with both the first half and the second half. That's a bit inefficient.

Our two rules about fill-in-the-blank items prefer this simple form with strong built-in guidance as to the type of answer wanted:

The most common gas in the Earth's atmosphere is _____.

More questions? See #71 and #73.

What Are the Characteristics of a Good True-False Question?

True-false items have some advantages. They can be written quickly and are very easy to link to specific instructional objectives of demonstrating knowledge. On the other hand, guessing the right answer for these sorts of items is pretty easy for students. After all, they have a 50/50 shot at getting the right answer without even reading the question. Consequently, if you plan to use true-false items, you should use a lot of them to cover each important content area. Another problem with true-false items is that they are surprisingly tricky to compose because, while it is easy to write statements that are undeniably false, it turns out that it is hard to write a statement that is undeniably true.

Because of the difficulties inherent in using true-false items, many advise that teachers not use them at all. If one does decide to use true-false items, however, researchers and measurement experts tend to agree that these guidelines should be followed:

---

1. Items should have simple structure.

Because of the difficulties in composing statements that are absolutely true without argument, keeping statements brief and to the point is a good idea.

---

2. Items should be entirely true or entirely false.

See Rule #1. Teachers don't want to get into arguments with bright students about whether a statement is "mostly true" and, therefore, "true" is the right answer. After all, a mostly true statement is actually false. Or is it? You can see the problem.

---

3. True and false statements should be of equal length.

Some students have learned that teachers often have to add all sorts of qualifying language to a statement to make it clearly true. So, length alone might be a predictor of the right answer in those cases.

---

4. There should be an equal number of true and false statements.

If students have a guessing strategy, they might benefit from a teacher with a tendency to mostly write true statements or mostly write false statements. Also, by covering both the ability to recognize truth and the ability to recognize falsehoods, a balanced approach would seem to be the most valid strategy for sampling that analytic ability.

More questions? See #70 and #71.

Can I Improve the Quality
of a Test After I Give It?

Of course, we probably wouldn't have asked the question if the answer was no! Yes, one can improve a classroom test after it is given and before final scores or grades are assigned. This is done by using item analysis information. Questions #36 and #37 demonstrate how to calculate item difficulty and item discrimination values for individual test questions. Real-life classroom teachers use that information to identify and remove "bad" items. Then, they rescore their tests. Bad test questions, under this approach, are either items that are too difficult or items that are negatively related to the total test score.

Some teachers worry about whether their tests are too hard. If there are questions that lots of students miss, maybe, the thinking goes, it wasn't taught well or wasn't covered. This way of thinking is consistent with a criterion-referenced philosophy, not a "just curve the test" norm-referenced approach (see Question #6).

Question #36 showed this formula for calculating item difficulty for individual questions:

$$\text{Item Difficulty} = \frac{\textbf{Number of People Who Got the Question Right}}{\textbf{Total Number of People Who Took the Test}}$$

The resulting proportion indicates how many students got the question correct. So, which difficulty indices are *good* and which are *bad?* Almost all teachers want, at a minimum, at least the majority of their students to get a question correct to be sure that the associated content was covered adequately. So an item difficulty index below .51 is a red flag that an item is "too hard." Most teachers who do item analyses want difficulty indices of, at least, .60. The logic of picking .60 or higher as a goal is that a test full of items that hard or harder would produce an average grade of D or F. Now, that's a hard test.

Items can also be identified as bad if they are related negatively with the total score. If they measure something different than the rest of the test does, the reasoning goes, they don't belong on the test. And if students who did well on the test were more likely to miss a question than those who did poorly on the test, the item is behaving strangely and should be removed from the test for that reason. Question #37 describes a practical formula (which doesn't require computing a correlation between each item and the total score) for the item discrimination index, which examines whether an item is tricky in this way. First, divide the completed tests into two groups—a high-scoring group and a low-scoring group—and then calculate the discrimination index this way:

**Item Discrimination Index = Difficulty Index in the
High-Scoring Group – Difficulty Index in the Low-Scoring Group**

Interpretation of this index for purposes of identifying bad items that should be removed from the test is pretty straightforward. Any value below 0 indicates that more people in the high-scoring group missed it than in the low-scoring group. That's a bad item.

To improve tests through item analysis, the easiest way is to score up the original tests, calculate the item analysis indices, and then count the total number of bad items. Next (and this isn't quite correct mathematically), most teachers simply add that number of points to *everyone's* score. So, if you missed it, you now get credit for it, and if you got it right, you get an extra point for it (which seems fair because it was extra tough). The only wrinkle to be careful of is to make sure no student gets more than the maximum points possible on a test.

More questions? See #35, #36, and #37.

I Want to Measure My Students' Skills and Ability. How Do I Design a Good Performance-Based Assessment?

The key to good performance-based assessment is in the scoring system. You need to be able to score the performance or product (see Question #70) in a way that is subjective enough for you to evaluate quality with high validity, but concrete enough that you can assign a score with good inter-rater reliability as described in Question #23. You also want there to be multiple components that are combined for a total score. That helps with reliability, as well. The key tool for both valid and reliable scoring of performance-based assessments is the **scoring rubric**.

Rubrics are an organized, written set of scoring rules, often in the form of a table. They identify the criteria and required parts and pieces for a high-quality (and high-scoring) response or product. Rubrics usually show the relative weights of the criteria and the pieces and the possible range of points for each.

Here's an example of a scoring rubric for giving a 4-minute speech:

	3 points	*2 points*	*1 point*	*0 points*
Introduction	Interesting opening. Topic is introduced. Main points are previewed.	Only two of the requirements were met.	Only one of the requirements was met.	None of the requirements were met.
Body	Three main points are presented.	Two main points are presented.	One main point is presented.	No main points are presented.
Conclusion	Interesting conclusion. Conclusion was signaled. Main points were summarized.	Only two of the requirements were met.	Only one of the requirements was met.	None of the requirements were met.

	3 points	*2 points*	*1 point*	*0 points*
Use of Time	Speech took between 3½ and 4 minutes.	Speech took between 3 and 3½ minutes or between 4 and 4½ minutes.	Speech took between 2 and 3 minutes or between 5 and 6 minutes.	Speech took less than 2 minutes or more than 6 minutes.

Here are the steps for creating a rubric for scoring a performance-based assessment:

Step 1. Identify the purpose of the assessment.

What is to be measured by the rubric?

What will the score represent?

Step 2. Determine the criteria for success.

What will a good performance look like?

What are the crucial indicators of quality in student "answers"?

Step 3. Design the scoring system.

Are the distinctions between each score meaningful?

Is each score well defined in observable ways that make sense?

More questions? See #69 and #70.

I'd Like to Use Portfolio Assessment in My Classroom. What Are the Guidelines for Doing That Well?

Portfolios are a purposeful collection of a student's work. They have grown in popularity, starting in the 1980s, as a way of presenting a fuller picture of student progress, development, and learning than traditional classroom assessment can. The idea is that portfolio assessment provides so much more information to students, teachers, parents, and administrators than a single score or letter grade ever could. Portfolios can provide both formative and summative assessment information (see Question #80 to learn about formative assessment). Portfolios provide samples of students' ongoing work over time (e.g., writing samples, projects, tests, and quizzes) and are most informative when students have commented on the quality of their own work. The most complete portfolios include examples of students' best work and their not-so-best work and allow for observation of growth and development over time.

From a measurement perspective, portfolios may have validity and reliability concerns, so they should be designed carefully. Choosing student work that is representative and can be compared meaningfully across time as a student develops is important for validity. Reliability concerns tend to stem from the subjective nature of the evaluation process, though this can be dealt with to some extent if rubrics are used or, at least, criteria for quality are well defined (see Question #78 for guidance).

Here are some characteristics of useful and effective portfolios:

- **They are student centered.**

  Good portfolios allow student choice over what to include, and their goal is to demonstrate growth and learning for the individual, not a group of students.

- **They are qualitative.**

  When used properly, portfolios cannot be summarized by a number, "score," or grade. (Though, unfortunately, this is often required administratively at some point.)

- **They provide a rich variety of products.**

  Portfolios should include creative products, traditional academic work, writing samples, and tests.

- **They reflect student work over time.**

  The goal of portfolio assessment is to make learning visible.

- **There are opportunities for reflective self-assessment.**

  Students can learn to evaluate their own portfolios.

More questions? See #71 and #78.

How Can Classroom Assessments Actually Increase Learning?

You might think that the only reason to test students is to measure how much they have learned. After all, teachers have to assign grades, districts have to report how well their schools are doing, and so on. This type of assessment, called *summative* by educators, has been the focus in educational measurement for a long time. A modern form of classroom testing, however, an approach called *formative* assessment, focuses on gathering data while teaching and learning are occurring. And formative assessment has been shown to actually *increase* learning in the same way that instruction does.

Formative assessment is all about giving accurate and frequent feedback to students (and to teachers) about their learning while instruction is still going on. Quality feedback allows students to judge the effectiveness of their practice or study efforts and, more important, to assess themselves regarding their own level of understanding. It helps students control their own learning.

For formative assessment to produce self-directed learners, the teacher must design self-assessments that have certain characteristics:

- Students must have a self-chosen goal. What level of quality do they wish for their composition? How many words per minute do they wish to type?
- The assessment feedback must provide information about where students are in relation to that goal. Progress must be possible.
- The information must be very narrowly specific to the goal or some key step in reaching that goal. General feedback about quality, such as "great work!" is not effective for improving performance.
- The feedback should suggest a particular change in behavior or strategy.

You'll know that formative assessment is going on in a classroom when you see a lot of questions between teachers and students during instruction, frequent quizzes, and mini-assessments that don't count toward grades, students collecting and analyzing data about their own performance, and students evaluating the quality of their work using a rubric or scoring guide created in a collaboration between students and their teacher. When used well, formative assessment supports students learning for their own reasons and evaluating the quality of their own efforts. Formative assessment helps students to learn from themselves.

More questions? See #40 and #71.

I Want My Tests to Be Authentic. What Does That Mean, and How Do I Accomplish That Goal?

Much of the testing in schools is artificial. Many of the assessment activities that occur in classrooms don't assess those skills required outside of the classroom, such as the ability to think critically or understand deeply or self-evaluate the quality of one's own work. And the format of most school testing is something you would only see in school, not in the real world. (Think of multiple-choice tests or spelling bees.) One can design tests, though, that are realistic in their format and mirror the tasks that are valued in actual occupations and useful in life after school. These sorts of assessments are described as *authentic*.

For many purposes, authentic assessments should be more valid than traditional paper-and-pencil formats. If they are situated in intrinsically interesting and complex real-life contexts and represent the thinking process that professionals (e.g., mathematicians, scientists, writers) use, then authentic classroom assessment is more likely to tap into those meaningful constructs of learning that teachers seek.

Researchers and education experts have identified these characteristics of assessment that make it authentic:

- **The task is performance based, cognitively complex, and realistic.**

  Performance-based assessments require demonstrations of ability and skill and are usually scored subjectively (see Question #78). Realistic means that the activity or task is something that one does in the real world, not just in the classroom.

- **Students defend their answer or product.**

  Often this is a formal presentation in front of other members of the learning community, such as students and parents.

- **Students might collaborate with each other or with the teacher.**

  In real life, much of the intellectual and creative work is done as part of a team.

- **Formative assessment is often part of authentic assessment.**

  See Question #80 to see how formative feedback can increase learning.

- **Scoring is criterion-referenced, the criteria are known by students ahead of time, and multiple indicators are used for scoring.**

The goal is to produce quality, not outperform other students. Part of authentic assessment involves self-evaluation as one works, and a shared understanding of what the indicators of quality are is essential.

More questions? See #40 and #71.

I Want My Tests to Be Valid for All of My Students. What Are the Universal Design Principles I Need to Follow?

The concept of *universal design* first appeared in architecture and engineering and was based on the goal of full accessibility to buildings and public spaces to everyone, regardless of their physical characteristics or disabilities. Think ramps at entrances, doorways that are wide enough for everyone, and signs and buttons that are easy to read whether English is your first language or not. The same goal of universal design has been adopted by many for education, including educational assessment.

Here are the general universal design principles as they apply broadly, whether to assessment, teaching, designing automobiles, or building Web sites:

- **Equitable Use**

  Access and use is the same for people with diverse characteristics.

- **Flexibility in Use**

  Accommodates a wide range of preferences and abilities.

- **Simple and Intuitive Use**

  Easy to understand regardless of experience, language skills, and so forth.

- **Perceptible Information**

  Communicates necessary information effectively regardless of users' characteristics.

- **Tolerance for Error**

  Minimizes negative consequences of unintended actions.

- **Low Physical Effort**

  Can be used efficiently and comfortably without fatigue.

- **Size and Space for Approach and Use**

  Appropriate size and space are provided.

Though these guidelines sound kind of "engineery," and they are, they translate rather well into classroom assessment terms. Instead of thinking of access as only meaning being able to physically use a tool correctly or enter a space, think of access as meaning that the same test is equally valid and useful for all students. Following researchers' suggestions, here is how those universal design principles can be interpreted for test design:

- **Same test for all.**

  The goal is that the same test form and format is used for every student without any modification.

- **Scoring is tied to construct only.**

  Points are awarded for knowledge, skill, or ability only, not for anything unrelated to instructional objectives.

- **Use words, phrases, and concepts common across cultures.**

  Avoid pop culture references, stereotypes, and, of course, offensive terms.

- **Design assessments so they could be easily adapted for different disabilities if necessary.**

  Use horizontal text. Avoid irrelevant graphics. Keys and legends should be at top or right of items. Avoid time limits.

- **Provide consistent and precise directions and instructions.**

  Provide sample or practice items. Number all items.

- **Maximize readability and comprehensibility.**

  Use simple, clear words. Clearly define technical terms. Use short sentences. Sequence instructions.

- **Maximize legibility.**

  Use off-white paper and black type. Avoid grayscale shading. The font should be at least 10-point with 12-point for graphics. Sans serif fonts are best. Use uppercase letters as answer options. Use left-justified text.

More questions? See #40 and #71.

PART 9

UNDERSTANDING TEST REPORTS

What Is the Normal Curve?

The normal curve is a very common shape for the distribution of scores. Measure almost anything in the natural world. Then, graph it so that the possible scores are ranked along a bottom X-axis and the frequency of scores is plotted along a vertical Y-axis. Provided that scores are allowed to vary and the level of measurement is at least at the interval level (see Question #3), the shape of that curve will be like a bell. The bell-shaped curve is well understood. So, the chances of a score occurring in any specific location under the normal curve are known. Even before you measure a group of people, you can predict how they'll score in terms of the normal distribution. Consequently, much interpretation in the world of measurement is in the context of the normal curve.

Here's what the normal curve looks like (SD means "standard deviation"):

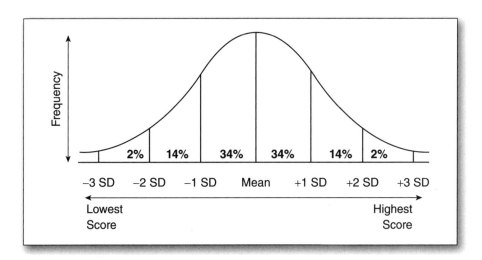

Notice these characteristics of the normal curve:

- The percentages shown in the figure are rounded off. 100% of all scores won't fit three standard deviations on either side of the mean. So, don't be misled; the curve actually goes on forever with scores further and further away from the mean always possible, but less and less likely.
- Most scores, about 68%, are within one standard deviation of the mean, and very few scores occur more than two standard deviations away from

the mean. Only about four out of 100 people will score more than two standard deviations above the mean or more than two standard deviations below the mean.

- It is symmetrical. Scores tend to occur above and below the mean with the same frequency.
- The mean is also the most commonly occurring score (the mode) and the point in the distribution where half the scores are above it and half the scores are below it.

Most standardized scores, such as IQ scores and SAT/ACT scores, are based on the normal curve. So, by knowing the mean and standard deviation of any standardized score and assuming scores are normally distributed, the likelihood of any possible score can be calculated.

More questions? See #84 and #85.

I See Percentile Ranks Reported
All the Time. What Are Those?

Maybe as a student, or maybe as a parent, probably both, you've all sat down with a teacher and had the results of an important standardized test shared with you. Among the variety of standardized scores often to be covered in these conversations are percentile ranks.

A percentile rank is *the percentage of people who scored at or below a given score*. So, if you received a percentile rank of 62, then you scored as well as or better than 62% of those who took the same test. Like most standardized scores, a percentile rank is norm-referenced (its meaning comes from comparing it to the average score), and its interpretation derives from assuming that scores are normally distributed. Notice, also, it is not the same as *percent correct* or the *percent of possible points* you received on a test. If most people got most questions right, you could actually do pretty good on a test, get an A, and still not have a very high percentile rank.

If scores are normally distributed, then the average score coincides with the 50th percentile. There are other key percentile ranks if one assumes that a normal curve describes the frequency distribution of scores from a test. How certain percentile ranks are related to the normal curve is shown in this table:

Point on the Normal Curve	Percentile Rank
Two Standard Deviations Below the Mean	2nd
One Standard Deviation Below the Mean	16th
Mean	50th
One Standard Deviation Above the Mean	84th
Two Standard Deviations Above the Mean	98th

By the way, there is another, less common, definition of percentile rank that says it is the percentage of people *below* a given score, leaving out the "at or below." For large groups of scores, this makes very little difference for interpretation. It does create the possibility of scoring at the 0th percentile rank, however. And it eliminates the possibility of receiving a percentile rank of 100. After all, you are among the total number of students, and you cannot score better than everyone if you are one of the everyones, but it is possible that no one scored less than you did.

More questions? See #83 and #86.

What Does It Mean to Say That a Test Is Standardized?

Y ou know those sorts of tests that are a big deal? They are those state-mandated tests, No Child Left Behind in reading, math, science, and social studies, to find out how much our kids are learning and how well our schools are doing. They are personality assessments that might be used to diagnose a mental illness. They are intelligence tests that will help to identify students who might be eligible for special education services. They are the college admissions tests such as the SAT, ACT, GRE, LSAT, and others that affect who gets into what university. These big deal tests are sometimes referred to as large-scale assessments, or high-stakes tests, or, *standardized* tests.

Technically, a test that uses a standard set of instructions and is administered in the same way to everyone who takes it is a standardized test. This definition, however, pretty much covers every assessment you can think of, from a classroom spelling test to that magazine quiz on whether you have the right stuff to attract Mr. Right. The way the term is normally used, though, it refers to a systematically constructed test that has been developed using scientific psychometric methods designed to produce a valid and reliable measure. The term also suggests a particularly informative type of scoring.

Here are the characteristics of a test that make it standardized:

- **Thoughtfully designed and constructed**

  The purpose of the test, the population for which it is intended, and the constructs or content areas to be measured are precisely defined up front. This guides the choice and format of the items or tasks that will make up the assessment and how they will be grouped to form useful scores and subscores. Typically, an iterative process of trying out items, collecting data on their properties, and revising the test is followed before a final version of the test is complete.

- **Administered following exact procedures**

  Standardized tests almost always have guidelines as to how much time is allowed, how test takers are allowed to behave during testing, and what security rules are in place during, before, and after testing. If the test is given one-on-one, the nature of the interactions between the administrator and the person taking the test is explicitly spelled out.

- **Produce an interpretable score**

  The scoring is usually objective, and any subjective scoring criteria are described carefully in a manual. Sometimes certified training is required for those tests for which the scoring is particularly subjective, such as with intelligence tests and some psychological measures. The scores themselves are typically *norm-referenced*, which means they are interpreted based on what the average score is. The term *standardized test* in some circles has become synonymous with *norm-referenced test* because of the standardized scores they produce.

  More questions? See #83 and #86.

What Is a Standardized Score, and Why Is It Important?

The raw score on a test actually means very little. That number at the top of a classroom quiz might indicate how many questions a student got right or, if slightly more informative, the percentage of questions he or she got right, but it doesn't tell us much about the level of the underlying construct that it is supposed to measure (e.g., knowledge). We don't know how hard the test was or how high most people score. Even the raw score from a scientifically developed instrument like the *Paranoia* scale on the *Minnesota Multiphasic Personality Inventory-2* (MMPI-2) provides hardly any guidance about one's level of paranoia. If we all have some level of paranoia, how much is too much? Consequently, to add information, raw scores from tests are often converted into *standardized scores*.

Standardized scores have been transformed from raw scores following known and standard rules, almost always based on what scores are normal or average. By knowing the rules, one can interpret performance in an agreed-upon way and identify levels of performance that are unusually high or unusually low.

The value of a standardized score comes from a philosophy that believes that significant scores are those that are not common. This *norm-referenced* approach is the dominant philosophy in medicine, psychiatry, and much of education. "We are all a little depressed from time to time, but you're more depressed than most people." "Yes, you only got an 82% on the final, but that was one of the highest scores in class, so you got an A." The alternative philosophy is a *criterion-referenced* approach, which believes that there are certain levels of performance or scores that have meaning, regardless of how the general population performs on the measure. "If you are this depressed, you should get treatment; it doesn't matter how many other people are as depressed as you." "You only mastered 82% of the material, and that's a B on my grading scale. In fact, no one in class got an A."

To create a standardized score, these steps are usually followed:

1. A large group of scores are collected from those who have taken the test.

2. The *mean* or arithmetic average is computed.

3. The *standard deviation* is computed. This is the average distance of each score from the mean and tells us about how much variability there is in performance.

4. Raw scores are converted to standardized scores by comparing the raw score to the average score and expressing the distance between them in terms of how far apart they are in standard deviations.

Common standardized scores include *Z*-scores, *T*-scores, IQ scores, SAT scores, and ACT scores.

More questions? See #83 and #85.

What Is a Z-score?

Z-scores are standardized scores that show in a single number how far above or below average a person scored. They are useful by themselves or as the first step in transforming a raw score into some other standardized score, such as an IQ score or SAT score.

The equation to calculate a Z-score is

$$Z = \frac{\textbf{Raw Score} - \textbf{Mean}}{\textbf{Standard Deviation}}$$

The math works in such a way that scores above the mean create positive Z's, and scores below the mean create negative Z's. Scores that are exactly average produce 0's as their Z-scores. It is the fact that the average Z-score is 0 (or *Zed* in British English) that gives it its name of Z.

Assuming that a group of scores follows the normal curve (see Question #83), Z-scores have these characteristics:

Z-scores		
Typical Range	Mean	Standard Deviation
−3.0 to +3.0	0.0	1.0

Z-scores are norm-referenced. A Z is interpreted by looking to see whether it is positive, which means it is above average, or if it is negative, which means it is below average. The quantity tells us whether it is close to average or unusually far away.

Imagine that three students, along with their classmates, took the same final exam. Fifty points were possible. For our example, assume the mean for the whole class (M) was 40 and the standard deviation (SD) was 6 points. The test scores for these three students and what their Z-score equivalents would be are shown in the table along with interpretations of what each value means.

▶ 163

Student	Test Score $M = 40, SD = 6$	Z-score	Interpretation
Bilbo	50	$50 - 40/6 = 1.67$	Far above average
Frodo	42	$42 - 40/6 = .33$	About average
Sam	30	$30 - 40/6 = -1.67$	Far below average

More questions? See #83 and #86.

What Is a *T*-score?

While the *Z*-score is a clever way to add meaning to raw scores by reexpressing them as a distance above or below the mean (see Question #87), they are a weird sort of number. *Z*-scores around 0 are perfectly good scores to get because they are average, and *Z*-scores can be negative (because half of all raw scores are below average). Parents, students, and teachers may not be comfortable with such a crazy distribution. *T*-scores were invented to place *Z*-scores on a less strange scale. Like a *Z*, *T*'s are standardized scores that show in a single number how far above or below average a person scored, but they cannot be negative, and even the lowest score will be greater than 0. They are reported for some standardized tests, such as the MMPI personality test discussed in Question #66. (As we talk about *T*-scores, don't confuse them with *t* values, used in statistical comparisons of groups. *T*-scores are single scores, while *t* values describe the difference between two group means.)

One begins with a *Z* and transforms it to a *T*. The equation to calculate a *T*-score is

$$T = 50 + (Z \times 10)$$

With these calculation rules, scores above the mean create *T*'s above 50, and scores below the mean create *T*'s below 50. Scores that are exactly average produce *T*'s of 50. This is a range of values that is easy on the eyes.

Assuming that a group of scores follows the normal curve (see Question #83), *T*-scores have these characteristics:

T-scores		
Typical Range	Mean	Standard Deviation
20 to 80	50	10

Like most standardized scores, *T*-scores are norm-referenced. A *T* is interpreted by looking to see whether it is greater than 50, which means it is above average, or if it is less than 50, which means it is below average. The distance from 50 indicates how far above or below the mean it is.

Using the data from our students presented in Question #87, let's see how raw scores become *T*-scores. It's a two-step process because we have to make *Z*'s along the way. In our example, the mean for the whole class (M) was 40, and the standard deviation (SD) was 6 points.

Student	Test Score $M = 40, SD = 6$	Z-score	T-score	Interpretation
Bilbo	50	$50 - 40/6 = 1.67$	$50 + (Z \times 10) = 66.70$	Far above average
Frodo	42	$42 - 40/6 = .33$	$50 + (Z \times 10) = 53.30$	About average
Sam	30	$30 - 40/6 = -1.67$	$50 + (Z \times 10) = 33.30$	Far below average

More questions? See #83, #86, and #87.

I Want to Understand How
I Did on the SAT. How Can
I Interpret My Score?

S AT scores are reported as standardized scores that range from 200 to 800, with 500 as the average score (see Question #42). You can interpret your score by comparing your score on a single test or the combination of all three tests—*Writing, Critical Reading,* and *Mathematics* (which have a mean of 1500 and a standard deviation of about 300)—with the mean score. A comparison of your score with the mean score is the interpretation that college admissions offices use. If the SAT is required as part of application materials, colleges use that norm-referenced information, along with lots of other data, to make decisions about whom to admit. They generally use the combined score for those decisions.

With a standard deviation of 100 for the standardized SAT score, about 68% of all test takers will be between 400 and 600. Assuming that scores are normally distributed, you can use our knowledge of areas under the normal curve (see Question #83) to figure out how common or rare any particular score is. For example, only about 4% of all test takers will get above 700 or below 300. The most prestigious universities have so many applicants that they usually require a minimum SAT score of 2100 (for the three-test combined score), which represents the top 10% of graduating high school students.

Question #92 explains that there is a certain amount of random error in test scores, and for the SAT, that typical error means that your true score (the average score you'd get if you took the same test many times) is within an interval of about 35 points above or below the score you received. Think of this as a guide to whether it is worth it to retake the test in hopes of getting a higher score.

Here are some key percentile ranks for the SAT. For each of these scores, the percentage of all test takers who get that score or less is shown. It varies a bit depending on which test you look at (and some scores have been approximated by rounding up or down):

Percentile Rank	Writing	Critical Reading	Mathematics
99th	760	760	790
90th	650	650	680

(Continued)

(Continued)

Percentile Rank	Writing	Critical Reading	Mathematics
75th	570	580	600
60th	520	530	550
50th	490	500	510
40th	460	470	480
35th	440	450	470

More questions? See #42 and #86.

How Can I Interpret My ACT Score?

ACT scores are reported as standardized scores with an official mean of 18 and a standard deviation of 6 (see Question #43). The possible range of scores is 1 to 36. Over time, performance on the ACT has increased, and these days actual scores on the test have resulted in a mean of about 20 and a standard deviation of about 4½. You can interpret your score by comparing your score on a single test with that mean of 20 or by looking at your average of all four required tests: *English, Mathematics, Reading,* and *Science.* A comparison of your score with the mean score is the interpretation that college admissions offices use. Colleges use that score, along with all the other information they ask for, to make decisions about whom to admit.

With a standard deviation of about 4½ for the standardized SAT score, we'd expect 68% of all test takers to score between 15 and 25. Assuming that scores are normally distributed, you can use our knowledge of areas under the normal curve (Question #83) to figure out how common or rare any particular score is. For example, only about 4% of all test takers will get above 29 or below 11. Top universities, like Ivy League schools, have so many applicants that they usually require a minimum ACT composite score of 28, which represents the top 10% of test takers.

Question #92 explains that there is a certain amount of random error in test scores, and for the SAT, that typical error means that your true score (the average score you'd get if you took the same test many times) is within an interval of about 2 points above or below the composite score you received, and between 3 and 4 points above or below the score for any individual test. Think of this as a guide to whether it is worth it to retake the test in hopes of getting a higher score.

Here are the key percentile ranks for the ACT. For each of these scores, the percentage of all test takers who get that score or less is shown. It varies a bit depending on which test you look at (and some scores have been approximated by rounding up or down):

Percentile Rank	Composite	English	Mathematics	Reading	Science
99th	33	35	34	34	33
90th	28	29	28	30	27
75th	24	24	24	25	24

(Continued)

(Continued)

Percentile Rank	Composite	English	Mathematics	Reading	Science
60th	22	22	22	22	22
50th	20	20	20	20	20
40th	19	18	18	19	19
35th	18	17	17	18	19

More questions? See #43 and #86.

I Took the GRE. What Does My Score Mean?

GRE stands for the *Graduate Record Examination,* or, at least, it used to. As with many of the tests produced by ETS, the large testing company, it is officially referred to only by its initials these days. The GRE is required as part of the admission materials for graduate school (e.g., master's and doctoral degree programs) at many universities.

If you took the test in the last few years, we are likely talking about the *GRE Revised General Test,* and you almost certainly took the test on a computer. This test is meant to assess the kinds of verbal, math, writing, and critical reasoning skills believed to be important for success in graduate school. While college admissions tests for undergraduate applicants tend to measure knowledge and achievement, admissions tests for graduate and professional programs (like medical schools, business schools, and law schools) emphasize the broadly useful abilities that support smart thinking across a variety of careers.

There are three sections on the GRE these days: *Verbal Reasoning, Quantitative Reasoning,* and *Analytical Writing.* For the reasoning tests, scores range from 130 to 170 and are meant to reflect your ability analyze, understand, and interpret written language and quantitative information. The *Quantitative Reasoning* section also expects you to demonstrate your math skills. For the *Analytical Writing* section, you are asked to write a complex essay in which you present and support an argument or position. On this writing test, scores range from 0 to 6. Question #44 gives more information about the content on the GRE.

For the reasoning subtests, the mean is around 151 with a standard deviation of about 7½. For the analytical writing test, scores go up in ½-point increments, with a mean of about 3.7 and a standard deviation of about 1. By assuming a normal distribution, you can interpret your score by comparing it with these average scores. For example, only about a sixth of all test takers score above 158 on the reasoning tests and above 4.5 on the writing test.

Here are the key percentile ranks for the GRE. For each of these scores, the percentage of all test takers who get that score or less is shown. You might note that scores are not quite distributed exactly like the normal curve. It varies a bit depending on which test you look at (and some scores have been approximated by rounding up or down, especially for the *Analytic Writing* section with its limited score range):

Percentile Rank	Verbal Reasoning	Quantitative Reasoning	Analytic Writing
99th	169	170	6.0
90th	162	164	5.0
75th	157	159	4.5
60th	154	155	4.0
50th	151	152	4.0
40th	149	150	3.5
35th	148	148	3.5

More questions? See #44 and #86.

What Is a Standard Error of Measurement?

Sometimes when testing experts report test scores, they will talk about how wrong the score might be. For many tests, instead of simply telling you your score, they will instead provide a range of values within which your actual ability level lies. This sort of hedging is particularly common when the person reporting results is a professional or is well trained in measurement. This person is correctly applying knowledge of the *standard error of measurement*.

Every test has its own standard error of measurement, which is mathematically determined based on the test's reliability. In Question #17, we talked about the reliability of test scores. The idea was that some of the variability of test scores was due not to actual differences among people, but just to some amount of chance that leads to a degree of randomness in individual responses. Well, that randomness, that amount of error that results in a score being a little higher or lower than it should be, is fairly well understood by measurement folks. The amount of error is assumed to be normally distributed. That is, it follows the normal curve (see Question #83). This means that we can make assumptions about how much error to expect on average.

A standard error is calculated using an equation that takes into account the *coefficient alpha* for a test (a commonly reported estimate of internal reliability; see Question #31) and its variability as summarized with a *standard deviation* (SD). Here is the formula for computing a standard error of measurement for a test:

Standard Error of Measurement =

Standard Deviation $\times \sqrt{1 - \textbf{Coefficient Alpha}}$

The standard error of measurement is the average distance between a person's score and the typical score he or she would receive across a large number of test administrations. Standard errors of measurement are usually reported in test manuals or on Web sites, or they can be calculated using this formula.

Using the necessary information, this table shows the standard error of measurement for a few imaginary tests:

Test	Standard Deviation	Coefficient Alpha	Standard Error of Measurement
Johnson Test of Cleverness	6	.80	2.68
Parsons Measure of Goofiness	10	.85	3.87
Woodson Arachnophobia Scale	15	.90	4.74

More questions? See #30, #46, and #93.

What Is a Confidence Interval?

*C*onfidence intervals* are the range of possible scores within which a test taker's *true score* probably falls. *True score* is the average score an individual
would get if he or she took the same test a large number of times (see Question
#17). Confidence intervals can be computed for different probabilities or levels of
"confidence" depending on how sure a test interpreter wants to be that the test
taker's typical level of performance is within a given range.

Confidence intervals can be built using a test's *standard error of measurement*, which was explored in Question #92. Assuming that standard errors are
normally distributed (which measurement experts do assume), we can choose
intervals associated with specific probabilities by assuming that the standard error
of measurement is the standard deviation of random errors around an observed
score (which measurement experts also do assume).

The thinking goes like this. If errors are randomly and normally distributed
around a true score, then observed scores close to the theoretical (and invisible)
true score will be very common, and observed scores far from the true score will
be rare. On a normal curve, 68% of scores are within one standard deviation of
the mean score, so 68% of the time observed scores should be within one standard
error of measurement of the true score. That's because the standard error of measurement is a standard deviation (of random errors) and the true score is a mean
score (of a theoretical infinite number of test-taking occasions).

Typically, those who use test scores want a greater confidence than 68%, and
they create confidence intervals larger than ± 1 standard error. They generally wish
to report a range of scores that will contain the true score 95% of the time, not
68% of the time, so they pick a larger number of standard deviations to build their
intervals. On the normal curve, 95% of values fall within 1.96 standard deviations
(to be precise) of the mean. Consequently, 95% confidence intervals around an
individual observed score are built by adding and subtracting 1.96 standard errors
to and from the observed score.

Here's the equation for a 95% confidence interval:

95% Confidence Interval = ±1.96 (Standard Error of Measurement)

Subtract this value from an observed score to get the lower end of the range
and add it to the score to get the higher end.

Using the same data we used in Question #92 to calculate standard errors of measurement, here are the distances to add and subtract from an observed score to create 95% confidence intervals for our imaginary tests:

Test	Standard Deviation	Coefficient Alpha	Standard Error of Measurement	95% Confidence Interval
Johnson Test of Cleverness	6	.80	2.68	± 5.25
Parsons Measure of Goofiness	10	.85	3.87	± 7.59
Woodson Arachnophobia Scale	15	.90	4.74	± 9.29

More questions? See #30 and #92.

PART 10

SURVEYS

What Is a Survey, and How Does It Work?

The term *survey* is actually used to mean a few different aspects of social science methodology, but all uses refer to a broad, general examination of something. *Survey* might refer to collecting data from a sample of people (or things) that are meant to represent a larger population, or it might refer to the questionnaire used to gather that data. For this book, we will focus on that second definition, the organized collection of questions that people call a survey.

Though surveys can include open-ended questions where respondents can say whatever they want, most surveys are designed to be analyzed quantitatively, with a selection of answer options offered to choose from for each question. Questions are written to be read by survey takers on paper or online or read to them in person or over the phone. In research, surveys are often used in political science, to assess public opinion, and in psychology, to explore the relationships among variables. Survey questions are asked to find out what people know, what they feel, and how they behave, and formats of questions vary depending on whether one is interested in facts, attitudes, or behaviors. Attitude survey formats are explored in Questions #62, #63, and #64.

Research design issues related to surveys center on the structure of the questions themselves, how items might be combined to measure key research variables, and the sampling methodology:

- Good survey questions should produce valid responses that reflect the actual underlying "true" answers as they apply to the person responding. Answers to survey questions should also be reliable and represent each individual's typical responses.
- Sometimes answers to questions are analyzed and reported individually, while other times research questions are best answered by summing or averaging responses across several related items that all measure the same broad *construct* (see Question #4).
- The sampling methods chosen are important for ensuring representativeness of survey responses when one wishes to generalize to a larger population than could be surveyed directly.

More questions? See #59 and #62.

I Need to Build My Own Survey. What Are the Characteristics of Good Survey Questions?

The quality of a survey is a function of the quality of the questions asked. While there are entire books full of guidelines for survey item construction, following just nine simple rules will go a long way toward creating a valid and reliable survey instrument.

Here are some sensible survey construction suggestions:

1. **Use simple wording.**

   Bad: *When you sit down for breakfast each morning, how often do you eat eggs?*

   Better: *How often do you eat eggs for breakfast?*

2. **Use appropriate vocabulary and phrasing.**

   Word your questions the way that your population talks and thinks.

3. **Avoid including more than one idea in a question.**

   Bad: *Do you think that eggs are healthy and tasty?*

   Better: *Do you think eggs are healthy?*

   Do you think eggs are tasty?

4. **Avoid negatively worded items.**

   Bad: *Do you agree or disagree that eggs are not good for you?*

   Better: *Do you agree or disagree that eggs are good for you?*

5. **Avoid the use of abbreviations.**

   Try not to use technical jargon from your field including abbreviations and acronyms.

6. **Avoid hypothetical questions.**

   Bad: *If the cost of eggs increased, how would you feel?*

   Better: *How do you feel about the cost of eggs?*

7. **Avoid the use of nonspecific quantitative adverbs.**

   Bad: *How often do you have eggs for breakfast?*

   1. Frequently   2. Sometimes   3. Rarely

   Better: *How often do you have eggs for breakfast?*

   1. 5 or more times a week   2. 1–4 times a week   3. Less than once a week

8. **Write questions with balanced answer options.**

   Bad: *How would you rate the taste of eggs?*

   1. Very Good   2. Good   3. OK   4. Bad

   Better: *How would you rate the taste of eggs?*

   1. Very Good   2. Good   3. Bad   4. Very Bad

9. **Avoid related questions; combine them into one question if possible.**

   Bad: *1. Have you ordered eggs at a restaurant?*

   1. Yes   2. No (If "No" please skip Question 2.)

   2. How would you rate the taste of eggs when you order them at restaurants?

   1. Very Good   2. Good   3. Bad   4. Very Bad

   Better: *1. How would you rate the taste of eggs when you order them at restaurants?*

   1. Very Good   2. Good   3. Bad   4. Very Bad

   N.A. I never order eggs at restaurants.

   More questions? See #59, #62, and #94.

How Do I Put Together a Generalizable Sample?

A generalizable sample is a group of people (usually) that fairly represents a larger group from which they were drawn. The idea is that we can measure that smaller group more easily than the larger group. The larger group is the population, and good samples represent the population in all important ways.

There are a variety of ways that researchers can build a sample, but it usually starts with the same four steps. Imagine that we wish to create a representative sample of U.S. schoolteachers. We'd follow this process to begin:

1. **Define the general universe.**

   This is the abstract population we wish to study. For our example, it would be

   U.S. schoolteachers

2. **Identify an observable working universe.**

   This is a more concrete version of our abstract population; a version of the population that we can actually get to. We might use

   Teachers who belong to national teacher organizations

3. **Choose the sampling unit.**

   What are the members of our sample? Whom will we measure?

   A single teacher

4. **Develop or find a sampling frame.**

   We need a list or organized grouping of people in our working universe. For example,

   Lists of e-mail addresses of members purchased from the National Education Association and the American Federation of Teachers

Next we sample from the sampling frame. There are different ways we can choose, though, and the different ways have different levels of generalizability. Here are the different methods of sampling:

- **Random**

  Random selection means every member of the population has an equal and independent chance of being selected. For our study, we might

  Number all e-mail addresses and randomly produce numbers.

- **Systematic**

  This means to move through the sampling frame in an organized predetermined way. We might

  Pick every 50th e-mail address.

- **Stratified random**

  You first identify subgroups in your population that you wish to represent in some predetermined proportional way and then sample from those subgroups. For example, we might

  Group teachers by teaching level—elementary and secondary—and then randomly select from each group.

- **Cluster**

  You randomly choose a larger unit that includes many of your sampling units and then include all members of that larger unit. Clusters are naturally occurring groups, and clusters may be chosen randomly, systematically, or through stratification. For example,

  Start with a working universe of all schools. Randomly select schools (each school is a "cluster" of teachers) and survey all teachers in that school.

These first four methods provide samples with adequate representativeness and are considered *probability sampling* approaches (because the probability of selection is known), with random selection being the best.

Two other common sampling methods do not do a good job of producing generalizable samples. They are *nonprobability* sampling approaches (so called because the probability of selection cannot be calculated):

- **Judgment**

  The researcher picks a sample that is believed to be "best."

  Recruit the teachers who appear to be in touch with today's issues.

- **Convenience**

  Probably the most common sampling approach, even among social scientists, is to start with a sample that is easy to obtain. For our study, a convenient sample would be produced if we

  Recruit the teachers in our school.

  More questions? See #8 and #94.

I've Got My Survey and a Sample. Now, How Do I Administer the Survey?

In the modern world, there are many different modes of survey administration. Surveys can be delivered in person, as an interview, over the phone, through the mail, and online through e-mail using computers or mobile devices. Quite a bit of research has been done on the best way to administer a survey, especially in terms of how to increase the response rate. Because the key to a useful survey study is to be able to generalize the results, getting as many people as possible to agree to fill out the survey and "return" it is critical. Much that is known about increasing response rate has been summarized by Don Dillman, a researcher and sociologist, who has published respected textbooks on survey methodology for decades.

The **Dillman method** is based on *social exchange theory*. This theory suggests that people will answer survey questions as part of a voluntary social interaction when

- rewards are perceived as high,
- costs are perceived as low, and
- trust is established.

Rewards for filling out a survey can be concrete or symbolic. Rewards can take the form of providing information about the survey, showing positive regard, thanking the respondent, asking for advice, and providing incentives (such as a small amount of money or a small gift).

Low costs can be established by avoiding demanding language (i.e., "You must respond!"), using easy-to-understand language, including a direct link to the survey (if the invitation is an e-mail) or a self-addressed stamped envelope (if it is an old-fashioned paper mail survey), and making the survey appear short and easy to complete.

Trust can be established when you assure and ensure confidentiality and security, provide a small token of appreciation, and secure sponsorship by an organization your population trusts, and when you put forth enough effort in constructing the survey to make the task appear important.

In addition to Dillman's advice to establish high reward, low cost, and trust, best practice in survey administration should follow these three key research findings:

- Multiple contacts are needed to achieve a high response rate.
- Incentives increase response rates.
- Surveys that appear easy to complete yield higher response rates.

More questions? See #8 and #96.

How Do I Report the Results of My Survey?

The results of a survey are reported in one of two ways: at the item level or as scale and subscale means across a group of items.

When you see the results of a survey on the TV news or in a newspaper, they're usually at the item level. That is, the responses for a single survey question are shown. For example, using an item from Question #95, results might look like this:

How often do you have eggs for breakfast?

8%   5 or more times a week

16% 1–4 times a week

76% Less than once a week

The frequency with which each answer option was chosen is reported as a percentage of the whole, and the percentages of all answer options total to 100.

You don't have to stick with the separate answer options as defined on the original survey; you can combine answer options if you'd like to make a point:

How often do you have eggs for breakfast?

24% At least once a week

76% Less than once a week

You can even condense the results more and turn the report into a single sentence, like a news headline:

This just in, chicken ranchers concerned that only 1 out of 4 of us eat eggs for breakfast at least once a week!

If the single item you'd like to report on is at a higher level of measurement than nominal or ordinal (see Question #3 for a discussion of levels of measurement), it might be more informative to report the mean score instead. So, for an item like this, where the answer options are coded or "scored" 1 through 4 and there are roughly equal distances in meaning between options (see Questions #63 and #64):

How would you rate the taste of eggs?

1. Very Good   2. Good   3. Bad   4. Very Bad

Instead of reporting the results this way:

How would you rate the taste of eggs?

34% Very Good

42% Good

18% Bad

6% Very Bad

you could report results this way:

Respondents were asked to rate the taste of eggs on a scale of 1 to 4, with 1 indicating "Very Good" and 4 indicating "Very Bad." The mean response was 1.96 or about 2. The average person believes eggs taste good.

There are benefits to producing a mean instead of just showing percentages for each response option. It is often easier to interpret and communicate results, and there are more powerful statistical techniques available for analyzing means instead of frequencies.

The second common way of reporting results from surveys, combining items, is typically the approach taken by researchers. Their goal is usually to measure an abstract construct such as attitude or a personality trait, and the best way to measure those sorts of invisible concepts reliably is by asking the question in different ways a number of times and combining all those multiple observations together into a single precise score. A mean works best here, instead of just summing the different responses. This can be done when all the items are at the interval level (that higher level of measurement described in Question #3) and use the same set of answer options.

More questions? See #3 and #63.

What Is the "Margin of Error" That Is Often Reported With Survey Results?

Question #92 describes the standard error of measurement, which is the average distance of each person's observed score from each person's true score. Other questions present the standard deviation of a group of scores, the average distance of each score from the mean score. In statistics, for most of our sample estimates (e.g., means, scores, correlations), we can figure out how close that estimate is on average to the correct estimate. Proportions and percentages are no different. Just as there is a standard error of measurement, there exists the **standard error of proportion**. The **margin of error** that is reported with many surveys on the news and in the media is about two standard errors wide.

For each percentage reported as part of a survey's results, we can figure out how close that estimate is to what we would find if we were to measure the entire population. Remember that surveys use sample results to infer to a larger population and often report results like this:

How often do you have eggs for breakfast?

At least once a week 24%

The standard error of proportion tells us, on average, how close that sample proportion (i.e., .24) is to the population proportion. The determining factors that affect precision of sample estimates are

- **Sample size**

  The larger the sample size, the more precise the estimate, and the smaller the standard error of proportion.

- **The observed percentage in the sample**

  The closer the estimate is to chance (i.e., 50%), the larger the standard error of proportion.

Here is the equation for the standard error of proportion (p = proportion):

$$\text{Standard Error of Proportion} = \sqrt{\frac{p(1-p)}{\text{Sample Size}}}$$

Statisticians typically want to know the range within which the population value will fall 95% of the time and, statistically, that will be about two standard error of proportions above or below the sample estimate, so to compute the "95% confidence interval" or "95% margin of error," we multiply the standard error of proportion by 1.96 (the mathematically exact value that gives us 95% confidence). Consequently, the equation for the margin of error is

Margin of Error = 1.96 (Standard Error of Proportion)

Using our *eggs for breakfast* example from this question, let's calculate the margin of error that would be reported. In our sample, 24% reported eating eggs for breakfast at least once a week, so our proportion of interest here is .24. Let's imagine that our sample size was 1,400.

$$\text{Margin of Error} = 1.96 \times \sqrt{\frac{p(1-p)}{\text{Sample Size}}}$$

$$\text{Margin of Error} = 1.96 \times \sqrt{\frac{.24(.76)}{1400}}$$

$$\text{Margin of Error} = 1.96 \times \sqrt{\frac{.1824}{1400}}$$

$$\text{Margin of Error} = 1.96 \times \sqrt{.00013}$$

$$\text{Margin of Error} = 1.96 \times .011$$

$$\text{Margin of Error} = .022$$

With this survey question and the associated margin of error of .022, or 2.2 percentage points, we would interpret results this way:

24% of our sample reported that they eat eggs for breakfast at least once a week. If we had been able to survey the entire population, we are 95% confident that somewhere between 21.8% and 26.2% would report that they eat eggs for breakfast at least once a week.

More questions? See #92 and #93.

What Are Common Mistakes Made in Survey Construction?

When researchers are putting together surveys for a study or, perhaps more commonly, when graduate students are designing a survey for their theses or dissertations, there are several errors that occur frequently. We will focus on three common mistakes that are easily avoided:

- **Unnecessarily using a variety of answer options**

  There is a tendency to create surveys with a bunch of items that, while somewhat related, all have their own individualized set of answer options. It is better to phrase all the items on a single scale as Likert-type attitude statements (see Question #63) with the same answer options. They can be answered more quickly and can be combined easily into a single scale score.

  Bad

  1. *How do eggs taste?*

     Awful   Bad   Okay   Good   Great

  2. *What is your feeling about how long it takes eggs to cook?*

     Takes too long   Takes some time   Eggs cook fast

  Better

  1. *Eggs taste great.*

     Strongly Disagree   Disagree   Agree   Strongly Agree

  2. *Eggs cook fast.*

     Strongly Disagree   Disagree   Agree   Strongly Agree

- **Requiring respondents to skip around**

  Taking a survey should be straightforward and linear, and it is troublesome when respondents are asked to skip questions or jump to different parts of a survey depending on their answers. Online surveys can be programmed to do this sort of skipping around seamlessly and invisibly, so that is an improvement over the traditional paper-and-pencil surveys, which used to require this. Even if this is done automatically by computer, though, interpreting results at the question level can become more difficult.

Bad

1. *Have you ever eaten at a restaurant that specializes in breakfast?*

   1. Yes   2. I Don't Know   3. No

   (If "I Don't Know" or "No," please skip to Question 3.)

2. *Which restaurants that specialize in breakfast have you eaten at?*

   _____

   _____

Better

1. *Which restaurants that specialize in breakfast have you eaten at?*

   _____I have never eaten at a restaurant that specializes in breakfast.

   _____

   _____

   _____

- **Measuring at the wrong level of measurement**

  Question #3 in this book describes the different *levels of measurement* and suggests that it is best when variables are measured in ways that provide as much information as possible. Sometimes this great piece of advice is forgotten when researchers write survey questions. This is commonly done when the answer to a question is a number. The highest level of measurement would allow respondents to enter any number, but, for some reason, survey developers often create predetermined categories of responses. This loses valuable information. Offering the full range of possible answers as choices allows for more powerful statistical analyses. One can always choose later to *report* the results grouped by interesting categories.

Bad

For about how many years have you worked at a restaurant?

0–1 years   2 years   3 years   More than 4 years

Better

For about how many years have you worked at a restaurant? _____

More questions? See #95 and #96.

Index

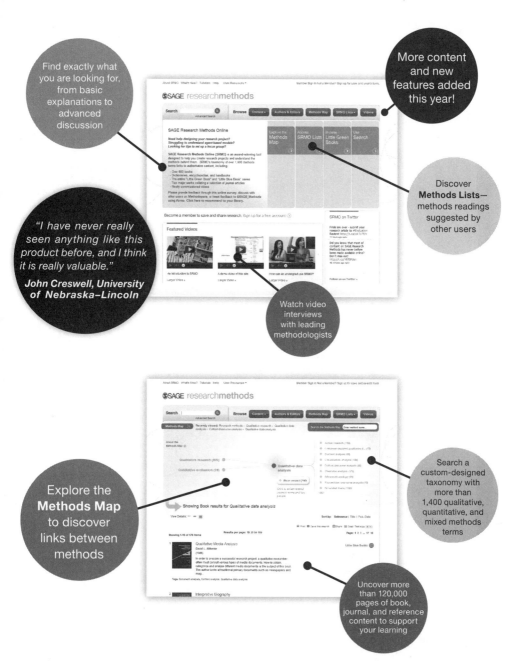

SAGE researchmethods

The essential online tool for researchers from the world's leading methods publisher

Find exactly what you are looking for, from basic explanations to advanced discussion

More content and new features added this year!

"I have never really seen anything like this product before, and I think it is really valuable."

John Creswell, University of Nebraska–Lincoln

Discover **Methods Lists**— methods readings suggested by other users

Watch video interviews with leading methodologists

Explore the **Methods Map** to discover links between methods

Search a custom-designed taxonomy with more than 1,400 qualitative, quantitative, and mixed methods terms

Uncover more than 120,000 pages of book, journal, and reference content to support your learning

Find out more at
www.sageresearchmethods.com